Museums of Philadelphia

Westholme Museum Guides

Museums of Atlanta
Museums of Boston
Museums of Chicago
Museums of Los Angeles
Museums of New York City
Museums of Philadelphia
Museums of San Francisco
Museums of Washington, DC

Visiting museums is one of the best ways to get to know a city. Westholme Museum Guides, designed for both residents and visitors, are the first-ever uniform compilations of permanent collections open to the public in America's major cities. Each city has its own unique group of museums, some famous, others practically unknown, but all of them are important parts of our nation's cultural life.

Museums of Philadelphia

A Guide for Residents and Visitors

Laura C. Waldron

WESTHOLME

Yardley

Acknowledgments
I wish to thank the many curators and staff who were so helpful in researching and preparing this book. I would also like to thank Laura Lindquist and Richard L. Franklin for providing helpful suggestions with the text, Christine Liddie for her copyediting, and John Hubbard for his beautiful cover design. And my love and thanks to my husband who encouraged the idea of this book.

Published by Westholme Publishing, LLC, Eight Harvey Avenue, Yardley, Pennsylvania 19067.

Maps by Joseph John Clark

10 9 8 7 6 5 4 3 2

ISBN 10: 1-59416-007-4

ISBN 13: 978-1-59416-007-3

www.westholmepublishing.com

Printed in the United States of America on acid-free paper.

For my father

Harold J. Waldron

Contents

Introduction

When William Penn first sailed up the Delaware River in 1683 to begin administration of the lands bestowed upon him by King James II, he selected a spot where a small Swedish settlement stood to found his capital city, Philadelphia. Here Penn would conduct his "Holy Experiment," in which religious and cultural liberality were not only practiced but were formally part of the legal code of the colony. With the streets of the city laid out within months of Penn's arrival — and many streets, parks, and other demarcations of Penn's original plan can be seen today — Philadelphia grew quickly and soon became the chief city in the American colonies. A city planned with a utopian vision of tolerance and inclusion naturally encouraged a heterogeneous society where cultures and castes mixed and borrowed, and within Penn's lifetime the colony of Pennsylvania would gain the reputation of being "the best poor man's country," where anyone had a chance to raise themselves up. Throughout its more than 300-year history, Philadelphia has always benefited from Penn's original ideals.

It was out of this vibrant community that the New World's first influential city arose. During the revolutionary and early national period, Philadelphia was second only to London in the English-speaking world. Nearly every major American figure of the time and many from abroad either lived here briefly or visited to attend the Continental meetings or for personal interests in commerce, art, or science. In fact, Philadelphia distinguished itself as a world-renowned center of science during this period, and it is for this reason that many of the collections profiled in this book have their origins at a time when the city was called the "Athens of America." The city was also a center of commerce and many merchants, especially Quaker ones, found their fortunes here, enabling them to construct elegant estates and furnish them with the finest material goods of the time. Some of these houses are now preserved as historic sites, while examples of their furnishings are in many of the collections of the city's museums.

Philadelphia in the eighteenth and early nineteenth centuries had a kind of draw on youth and those seeking fortune or a change of life the way New York City attracts talented people today. In Philadelphia, one of those rare instances occurred involving the serendipitous combination of a fertile community and a remarkable person. Benjamin Franklin came to Philadelphia from Boston in 1723. From that time on, the city and this man — one of the period's greatest scientific and progressive minds — would transform the world, culminating in the establishment of the first democratic nation. Franklin's beneficial influence on the city of Philadelphia is not easily exaggerated; he is everywhere. The American Philosophical Society, The Library Company, Pennsylvania Hospital, The Philadelphia Contributionship for the Insurance of Houses from Loss by Fire — all of these institutions and the similar ones they inspired world wide owe a debt to his interests and influence. In addition to civic and social programs, Franklin pursued his scientific studies here, corresponding with scholars throughout the world and close to home, including John Bartram, whose interest in native plant life Franklin encouraged. Remarkably, Bartram's actual estate remains in the city and is now a fascinating museum. Franklin's hand is also found in the shaping of the documents we hold dear as a nation, including the Declaration of Independence and the Constitution.

For those first-time visitors, a trip to Independence National Historical Park should be top priority, as it offers one of the most valuable interpretations of our nation's beginnings. Called "America's most historic square mile," Independence Mall, as it is known locally, has eschewed the kind of commercialization and theme-park designs that can elevate entertainment over education, and therefore visitors can enjoy many historic sites in this vicinity in the context of a thriving urban setting. Nearby Elfreth's Alley, for instance, has remained primarily a residential street with few noticeable changes over the course of centuries. Around the Mall you will find a number of important collections, many housed in historic buildings—the Betsy Ross House, the National Constitution Center, Fireman's Hall, the Atwater Kent Museum, Mother Bethel Church—that are easily within walking distance. And walking around the distinctive Old City and Society Hill neighborhoods is one of the pleasures of visiting this city. On some streets you can walk on the same stones tread at the time of the Continental Congress. As this book shows, there are museums with collections representing an extraordinary range of interests—toys, Civil War uniforms and weaponry, fine art, books, furniture, clothing—as well as an outstanding variety of architectural styles that radiate from Independence Hall in all directions, and these museums outside of the historic districts should be part of anyone's itinerary while here.

Of the collections representing the colonial and early republic periods, some of the most important are the historic house museums. Philadelphia has an extensive array of preserved houses open to the public, the largest number in the country, in fact. Because of Penn's prescient city design, including more green space than any other city before or since, wider streets, the common use of brick in building construction, and the early organization of the nation's first volunteer fire companies, a devastating fire never affected Philadelphia. As a result an exceptional proportion of colonial and Federal architecture survived into the twentieth century, and many buildings and private residences have been preserved, primarily through civic efforts. The densest concentration of museum houses is in Fairmount Park, a short drive from downtown. In the eighteenth century, this was the site of country houses for those who had the wherewithal to build retreats from the city. In addition, the yellow fever epidemics of the 1790s that killed nearly a third of Philadelphia's population resulted in even more people establishing households away from the urban center. The historic houses in Fairmount Park are, individually, national treasures, full of idiosyncratic family histories and decorative tastes, and as a group, a valuable resource for understanding architectural method and style, American and local history, and social and cultural practices of the times. The Philadelphia Museum of Art, which administers the park houses, sponsors trolley tours that are ideal for groups or for those who don't want to drive themselves to these locations. Both residents and visitors should make an effort to enjoy these special museums.

Germantown is also an important center of museums and historic houses, and there are a number—such as Cliveden or the Ebenezer Maxwell Mansion—that can provide a highlight to any visit to the city. Germantown, originally a separate town that was incorporated into Philadelphia in 1854, and the adjoining community of Chestnut Hill, can be easily reached through the local train system. Germantown was the site of a revolutionary war battle and the first Mennonite community and was briefly the capital of the United States when George Washington resided here. In addition to the Georgian, Federal, and Victorian house museums, the Germantown Historical Society is alone worth the short ride. As historic houses can be found in every part of the city, from Powel House in Society Hill to Glen Foerd along the Delaware River in Northeast Philadelphia, enjoying at least one should be on everyone's touring agenda.

Benjamin Franklin's worldwide reputation as a scientist and the city's vibrant intellectual community ensured that Philadelphia was the center of American scientific inquiry, and as a result there are a large number of world-class science museums in the city. Many of the institutions founded in the eighteenth and early nineteenth centuries continue to support and lead in scientific studies. The Academy of Natural Sciences is the nation's first natural history museum and remains an important center for biological and ecological research — in addition to being a great place to learn about dinosaurs — while the American Philosophical Society, founded by Franklin and full of fascinating mechanical devices, artworks, and other important historical artifacts, continues to provide research grants and awards for scientific achievement. The College of Physicians of Philadelphia opened in 1787 and is home to the Mütter Museum — famous for its important collection of rare medical artifacts — while the Wagner Free Institute of Science, founded in the mid-nineteenth century to provide free scientific education to the public, continues this mission today. Whether it is the wonderful aerodynamics exhibit at the Franklin Institute or the stunning artifacts from the ancient Near East at the University of Pennsylvania Museum of Archaeology and Anthropology, science museums in Philadelphia are among the most satisfying for families, those with curious minds, or those who simply enjoy seeing something unique, strange, or shocking—and returning home to share the experience with friends.

Given the general atmosphere of religious toleration provided by the Quaker leadership, Penn's Philadelphia attracted numerous religious groups, and many of the world's major religions have places of worship here. Several of these are important historically, and some are now museums or contain separate museums open to the public. In Philadelphia, you can visit St. George's, the oldest continuously used Methodist church in the world; the first Mennonite meeting house, located in Germantown; the Mother Bethel African Methodist Episcopalian church, founded by Richard Allen; the Philadelphia Museum of Judaica at Rodeph Shalom, which contains hundreds of ritual pieces; and the Arch Street Friends Meeting House, which gives a glimpse of early Quaker worship.

Philadelphia is, of course, a history-lover's dream. It is the site of our nation's birth, and many of the key buildings and artifacts associated with that event remain to be seen today. But the city offers lots of other opportunities for historical exploration in addition to the sites surrounding the American Revolution and the great house museums. Here in Philadelphia we have two important Civil War collections: the Grand Army of the Republic Museum and The Civil War Library and Museum, both of which contain singular artifacts that are sure to delight students of that war. We also have Eastern State Penitentiary, an imposing early prison; the house where Edgar Allan Poe rented rooms for his family and penned some of his most well-known stories; Fireman's Hall with its great collection of fire trucks and firefighting equipment; the Concord School House in Germantown, which allows visitors to see the conditions of education in the eighteenth century; and the African American Museum in Philadelphia and the National Museum of Jewish History, both of which document the centuries-long histories of these peoples in America.

The Philadelphia region has always embraced contemporary artistic expression. The local Pew Fellowships in the Arts, for example, remains at the leading edge of supporting creativity in all areas of the arts. The world-renowned Philadelphia Museum of Art provides an exceptional opportunity to experience works by past modern masters such as Duchamp, Dali, and Miró. That museum is, of course, the most famous in Philadelphia and deserves its status as "essential" when considering what cultural activities to enjoy in the city. Off the usual tourist path are many contemporary art centers and museums like the Fabric Workshop and the Wood Turning Center, dedicated to media and techniques not often represented by stand-alone collections. Artistic expression is entwined with social expression, so at the Living Loft Puppet Museum, for example, visitors can learn how puppetry has been used for centuries as a vehicle to enact social change, and at the National Liberty Museum, modern glass sculptures are on display as metaphors for the fragile nature of liberty.

The colonial and Federal eras are certainly present in Philadelphia, but the city has, true to its origins, kept its vibrancy and cultural mix. The characteristic red brick of Philadelphia buildings may have mellowed, but the vigor and variety of this "Holy Experiment" have not. Even long-time residents will be surprised at the range of the collections listed in this book. There is a shoe museum, a dental museum, and museums dedicated to dolls, books, insects, and even beauty. There are historic ships, great military collections, artwork by artists from every period and every culture, sports museums, and museums designed for children and families. There are important museums, many with libraries and research facilities, dedicated to the history and cultures of people from around the world who have made Philadelphia their home. Even the city's traditional New Year's Day revelers, the Mummers, have a museum that showcases how the long history of contact among various ethnic groups and cultures in the city gave rise to this quintessential Philadelphia tradition. Many times we use the term "museum" as shorthand for discussing a fine-art collection, but in these pages there are museums dedicated to history, science, hobbies, and immigrant cultures.

But what is a museum? For the purpose of this book, a museum is defined as a permanent collection, open to the public, of predominantly nonreproduction artifacts. Drawing such a distinction means, necessarily, that there are some important destinations that are left out. There are historic houses and major art galleries that despite sometimes being referred to as museums were nonetheless not included. Also not covered are other important destinations that will complement any visit to Philadelphia's museums such as the Philadelphia Zoo (the nation's first), the Morris Arboretum, and the Horticulture Center in Fairmount Park. There are several stand-alone pieces of public art that are not included in this guide that you will pass as you travel from one museum to the next. Any visitor or resident should take time to see the magnificent mosaic *Dream Garden* designed by Maxfield Parrish and accomplished by Louis Comfort Tiffany mounted in the lobby of the Curtis Building at the western edge of Independence Mall, the Robert Indiana LOVE sculpture in JFK Plaza, and Claes Oldenburg's *Clothespin* on Market Street near City Hall.

Visiting museums is one of the best ways to get to know a city, and Philadelphia has an enormous number and variety to enjoy. To visit a city's museums and their collections is to understand that city's history, values, and current concerns. It is also an experience that can be profoundly intimate, when you encounter the houses, belongings, or ephemera of those who have made Philadelphia their home over the centuries. If you are a visitor, try to make time to see some of the unique places profiled in this book. For residents, this will be a way of discovering more about what your city offers. It is also an opportunity to share the city with friends who come to visit.

Using *Museums of Philadelphia*

The 110 museums in this guide are listed in alphabetical order by the primary name of the museum or collection. Each entry provides the address, phone number, and Web site for the museum as well as when the museum is open and its admission prices and policies. Please note that this information can change, so it is best to confirm before you go, especially with the smaller museums that are often dependent on volunteer help. Calling ahead will inform you about special events, temporary exhibits, and any exhibition that may require additional ticketing. Many museums do not charge an admission fee, but donations are always welcome even when one is not suggested.

Each entry also features symbols to provide quick reference, such as whether a museum has exhibits for children, whether it is best to provide your own transportation, or whether you must call before visiting. A key to all of these symbols is at the end of this section.

Each museum is indicated on the maps by its page number, making it easy to find which museums are located near each other. Philadelphia has a well-developed public transportation system, and many museums, especially the ones associated with the colonial era, are within walking distance of Center City (what Philadelphians call their downtown), so visiting most collections does not require a private car or taxi. Calling a museum, consulting with the Independence Visitor Center, or speaking with a SEPTA agent will allow you to find public transportation or the best driving route to a particular destination.

Following the final museum entry is a section that lists the museums by different categories, such as the essential museums to see on a short trip, those most interesting to teenagers, and the major museums for history, art, or science. These are designed to give some guidance in planning your visit.

Further Reading and Resources

Klein, William M. *Gardens of the Delaware Valley*. Philadelphia: Temple University Press, 1995.

Moss, Roger W. *Historic Houses of Philadelphia*. Philadelphia: University of Pennsylvania Press, 1997.

Nash, Gary. *First City*. Philadelphia: University of Pennsylvania Press, 2001.

Weigley, Russell F. *Philadelphia: A 300-Year History*. New York: W. W. Norton & Co., 1982.

Visitor Information

Independence Visitor Center

One North Independence Mall West
6th and Market Streets
Philadelphia, PA 19106
800-537-7676 or 215-965-7676
visitor@independencevisitorcenter.com
www.independencevisitorcenter.com
Open: M–Sa, 8:30 AM–7:00 PM

The center provides information on accommodations, dining, shopping, transportation, and attractions in the city. The center has an ATM, restrooms, and light refreshments and offers maps, ticketing for attractions, listings of regional events updated daily, multilingual staff, and specialists who can provide one-on-one planning for your visit. There is underground parking at 5th and 6th Streets between Market and Arch Streets, open 24 hours a day. Maximum vehicle height clearance is 6' 6". Parking is also available at the National Constitution Center, 5th and Arch Streets.

Independence Hall Association

This volunteer organization was founded in 1942 and helped establish Independence National Historical Park. They now operate a dynamic Web site, **www.ushistory.org**, that provides an outstanding virtual tour of historic sites in the Philadelphia region.

Greater Philadelphia Tourism Marketing Corporation

30 S. 17th Street, Suite 1710
Philadelphia, PA 19103
215-599-0776
www.gophila.com

Historic Philadelphia, Incorporated

123 Chestnut Street, Suite 401
Philadelphia, PA 19106
215-629-5801
www.historicphiladelphia.org

These companies also provide information on making the most of your visit to the city. Their Web sites are particularly helpful for trip planning.

Regional Transportation

As noted, most museums in this book are accessible by foot from any of the hotels in Center City. Even the Philadelphia Museum of Art, despite a distance of just over a mile from the Convention Center, perhaps the furthest walkable destination from Center City, affords the visitor a delightful tour past public sculpture, important buildings, the Logan Circle, and the length of the Benjamin Franklin Parkway, modeled on Les Champs-Elysées, Paris, and is best enjoyed on foot. There are three main regional rail stations serving Center City at 30th Street Station (which is also a major Amtrak hub), Suburban Station, and Market East. All three are marked on the maps. Both Germantown and Temple University are readily accessible by rail.

SEPTA (Southeastern Pennsylvania Transportation Authority)

1234 Market Street

Philadelphia, PA 19107

215-580-7800 or 215-580-7853 (TDD/TTY)

www.septa.org

Maps and schedules for all regional rail, subway, and bus lines are available in printable form from the SEPTA Web site. Agents are also available for schedule information by phone, M–F, 6:00 am–8:00 pm; Sa & Su, 8:00 am–6:00 pm. During all other hours, an automated service is available.

Maps

Each museum in this book is marked on the following maps by its page number. These maps are designed to show the reader the general proximity of the museums to one another.

Museums of Philadelphia

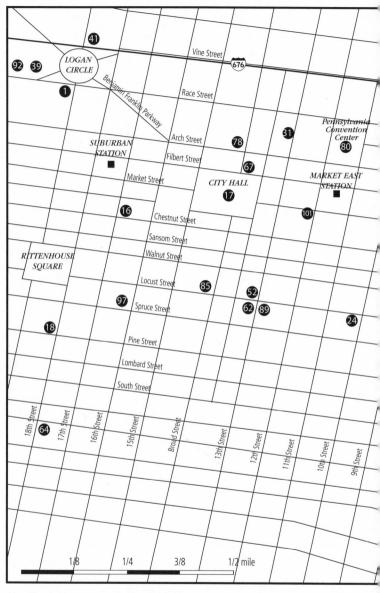

Map No. 1: Museums in Center City. (Each number is a museum's book page.)

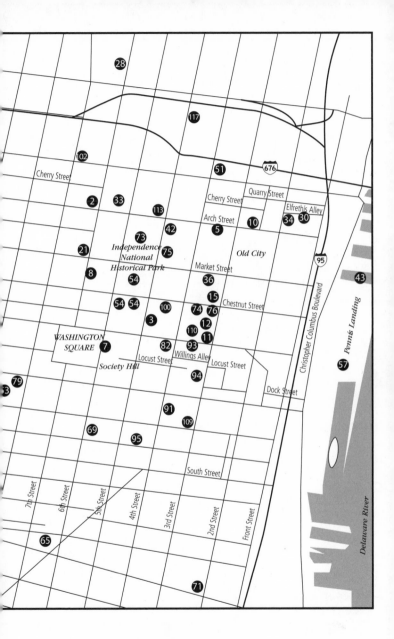

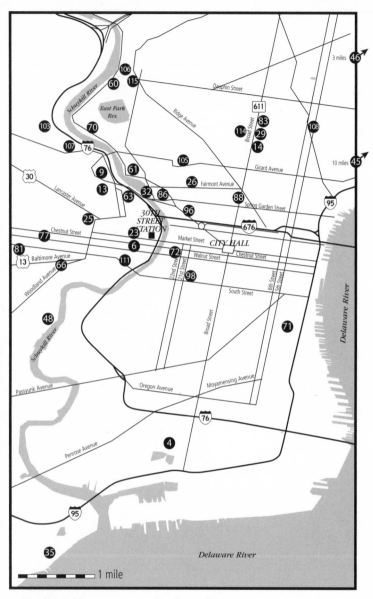

Map No. 2: Museums surrounding Center City

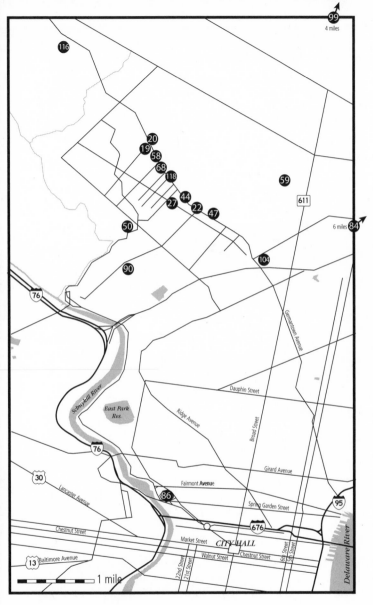

Map No. 3: Museums in the Germantown area

Visual Codes

Architecturally significant

Best to provide own transportation

Exhibits suitable for children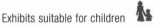

Food on premises

Must call ahead

Notable art

Notable grounds or garden

Science oriented

Site of historic event

The Academy of Natural Sciences

1900 Ben Franklin Parkway (Map No. 1)
215-299-1000
www.acnatsci.org

Open: M–F, 10:00 AM–4:30 PM; Sa & Su, 10:00 AM–5:00 PM
Admission: Adults, $8.50; Children, $7.50; Seniors, $7.75

Where else can you see the care of live wild animals, a skeleton of the largest meat-eating dinosaur, and a tropical rain forest full of real butterflies? At America's oldest natural history museum, of course. Founded in 1812, the Academy's scientific collections contain over 17 million specimens, ranging from dinosaurs to rare plants. Its present home was built in 1876 for the Centennial Exposition. In Dinosaur Hall visitors can see movies and computer videos, touch objects, and get up close to reconstructed skeletons and models, including *Tyrannosaurus rex* and *Gigantosaurus*. Other permanent collections include a hall of exquisite natural habitat dioramas, the Live Animal Center, and an extensive crystal and gem collection. Temporary exhibitions, many featuring objects from the Academy's vast holdings, are also always on display. It's worth noting that in addition to being a leading scientific research center, the Academy's Ewell Sale Stewart Library is American's oldest operating biological library and holds extensive written and photographic records of expeditions and voyages of discovery, including those led by Captain James Cook, John C. Fremont, and Ernest H. Shackleton.

Highlights:
The first dinosaur skeleton discovered in North America
John James Audubon's bird specimens

African American Museum in Philadelphia

701 Arch Street (Map No. 1)
215-574-0380 x228
www.aampmuseum.org

Open: Tu–Sa, 10:30 AM–5:00 PM; Su, noon–5:00 PM
Admission: Adults, $8.00; Children, Seniors, and Students, $6.00

The first museum dedicated to the history and accomplishment of African Americans to be founded by a municipality, the African American Museum in Philadelphia is dedicated to collecting, preserving, and interpreting the material and intellectual culture of African Americans in Philadelphia and the Americas. Built for the Bicentennial in association with the Smithsonian Institution on land that was once part of a historic black community, the museum tells the story of the African kingdoms that were destroyed by the slave trade, the fate of Africans in the new world, emancipation, and present-day civil rights movements and achievements. Viewers can learn about the arts and material culture of African craftsmen, the slave trade throughout the entire Western Hemisphere, abolitionists, and the history of organizations like the NAACP.

Highlights:
The Jack T. Franklin Photographic Collection—nearly half a million photos of African American life in Philadelphia

American Philosophical Society

104-105 S. 5th Street (Map No. 1)
215-440-3400
www.amphilsoc.org

Open: W–Su, 10:00 AM–4:00 PM (Mar.–Sept.); Th–Su, 10:00 AM–4:00 PM (Sep.–Mar.); M–F, 9:00 AM–5:00 PM (Library Hall)
Admission: Free

America's first learned society, founded in 1743 by Benjamin Franklin, has advanced "the promoting of Useful Knowledge" for more than 260 years. Its first ventures ranged from charting the course of the planet Venus to assisting the Lewis and Clark expedition. (Their original notebooks are here.) The American Philosophical Society continues to support scientific inquiry and can claim 230 Nobel prize winners in its history. There are two venues for exhibits open to the public: Library Hall and Philosophical Hall. Exhibitions in Library Hall, across the street from Philosophical Hall, feature pieces from the library's extensive collections, while Philosophical Hall exhibitions focus on history, science, and the arts. Here visitors can wonder at rare telescopes, clocks, surveying equipment, weather instruments, and other practical and curious devices. There are also a number of important early American paintings, including Gilbert Stuart's famous portrait of George Washington. This collection, like those at the Rosenbach and the Wagner museums (see below), is so full of interesting, famous, and surprising objects that any visitor should take the time to enjoy the offerings.

Highlights:
The armchair in which Thomas Jefferson wrote the Declaration of Independence

American Swedish Historical Museum

1900 Pattison Avenue, FDR Park (Map No. 2)
215-389-1776
www.americanswedish.org

Open: Tu–F, 10:00 AM–4:00 PM; Sa & Su, noon–4:00 PM
Admission: Adults, $6.00; Seniors, Students, and Children 12–18,
$5.00; Children under 12, Free

Swedes were the first permanent colonists of the Philadelphia
area, and their history and accomplishments are highlighted in
this homage to the home country and the early Swedish settlers.
First conceived in the early part of the twentieth century, the
museum gives a complete and fascinating account of the history
of Swedish Americans, from the New Sweden Colony, first
established in 1638, to the Swedish immigrant experience in the
American Midwest, to famous Swedes such as eighteenth-century botanist and explorer Peter Kalm, the brilliant engineer and
designer of the Civil War ironclad *Monitor*, John Ericsson, and
Jenny Lind, the nineteenth-century "Swedish songbird."

Highlights:
Early maps of the New Sweden Colony
A room devoted to the Nobel Prize
Artifacts from the first Swedish settlements
Recreation of a nineteenth-century Swedish *stuga* (farmhouse)
interior

Arch Street Friends Meeting House

320 Arch Street (Map No. 1)
215-627-2667
www.archstreetfriends.org

Open: M–Sa, 10:00 AM–4:00 PM
Admission: Free

Built in 1804 and enlarged in 1811, Arch Street is the oldest
Friends meeting house still in use in Philadelphia and the largest
in the world. In the nineteenth century men met on one side and
women on another; now the whole congregation shares the west
wing, which retains its peaceful, unadorned aspect. The east wing
houses a collection of Quaker artifacts from the formative years
of Philadelphia. Many Philadelphia notables were Quakers and
met here, not the least of which was Edward Hicks, painter of
the iconographic series, *The Peaceable Kingdom*. The beautifully
austere pillared brick building is raised above street level because
it was built on the site of a graveyard established by William
Penn in 1701; many of those buried underneath were victims of
the yellow fever outbreaks that plagued the city in the 1790s.

Highlights:
A "modesty board" running along the base of the staircase
reserved for girls
A piece of the treaty elm believed to be from the tree where
Penn conducted his famous contract with the Indians in 1682
An eighteenth-century funeral sleigh

Architectural Archives at the University of Pennsylvania

Kroiz Gallery, Fisher Fine Arts Building (Map No. 2)
220 S. 34th Street
215-898-8323
www.design.upenn.edu/archives

Open: M–F, 9:00 AM–5:00 PM
Admission: Free

The core of this archive is the Louis I. Kahn collection, a group of drawings, sketches, plans, correspondence, and photographs of the works of the school's most famous architecture alumnus. The collection has grown, however, to represent more than three centuries of architectural drawings, photos, and models by more than 400 architects and designers. The museum itself is housed in the ground floor of a building designed by Frank Furness, whose work is also represented in the archives.

Highlights:
Robert Venturi models
Robert Adam drawings
The Frank Lloyd Wright collection

Athenaeum of Philadelphia

219 S. 6th Street (Map No. 1)

215-925-2688

www.philaathenaeum.org

Open: M–F, 9:00 AM–5:00 PM (Gallery only); for building tours, please call for an appointment

Admission: Free

Founded in 1874, the Athenaeum is the home to a learned organization, a library holding almost half a million pieces from the architectural history of America, including drawings, photographs, and manuscripts, and an important collection of fine and decorative arts primarily from the period of 1800 to 1850. Gallery space on the first floor features temporary exhibitions on architecture and design that regularly showcase objects from the Athenaeum's collection. In the reading rooms of this Italianate Revival–style building designed in 1845 by John Notman, exquisite furniture and artworks are displayed, but visitors must call ahead for a tour.

Highlights:

Furniture and art from the collection of Joseph Bonaparte, older brother of Napoleon

Atwater Kent Museum of Philadelphia

15 S. 7th Street (Map No. 1)
215-685-4830
www.philadelphiahistory.org

Open: Daily, 10:00 AM–5:00 PM. Exhibitions closed Tu
Admission: Adults, $5.00; Seniors and Children 13–17, $3.00; Children 12 and under, Free

Named for the radio pioneer who bought this early-nineteenth-century Greek Revival building to save it from destruction, the Atwater Kent Museum showcases the history of the city of Philadelphia, but its scope continues to increase. With recent acquisition of holdings from both the Norman Rockwell Museum and the Historical Society of Pennsylvania, the Atwater Kent now represents one of the most extensive collections of Pennsylvania history and general Americana in the country. Exhibits are chosen from the museum's holdings of over 100,000 objects illustrating the growth and development of Philadelphia, the state of Pennsylvania, and the early nation, ranging from sports to science.

Highlights:
William Penn's wampum belt
Walk on the world's largest map of the city in the "Experience Philadelphia!" gallery
Religious Society of Friends (Quaker) clothing, household items

Belmont Mansion

2000 Belmont Mansion Drive, West Fairmount Park (Map No. 2)

215-878-8844

www.philaparks.org/ewaabm.htm

Open: Tu–F, 10:30 AM–5:00 PM. Weekends by appointment.
Admission: Adults, $5.00; Children, $3.00

The "country retirement" of William Peters, this impressive
mid-eighteenth-century Georgian mansion overlooks the
Schuylkill River and provides some of the best views of the city
of Philadelphia. One of the first Palladian structures in the
colonies, its landscaped grounds once encompassed miles. With
the coming of the American Revolution, Peters, a Loyalist sup-
porter, returned to England in 1768 and left the property in the
possession of his son, Richard, who was an important patriot,
holding such offices as Secretary of the Board of War for the
Revolutionary Army and Pennsylvania Delegate to Congress
under the Articles of Confederation. As a consequence of his
stature, Belmont Mansion provided hospitality to Washington,
Adams, Jefferson, Madison, and Lafayette. Later in its history,
the house provided a safe haven for escaped slaves heading north.
The house's original interior plaster and woodwork represent
some of the finest early examples remaining in the United States.
The house has recently received a major grant for its restoration
and will be closed for a period in the near future.

Highlights:
Elaborately paneled and carved woodwork and molded plaster
ceilings

Betsy Ross House

239 Arch Street (Map No. 1)
215-686-1252
www.betsyrosshouse.org

Open: Daily, 10:00 AM–5:00 PM (Apr.–Sep.); Tu–Su, 10:00 AM–5:00 PM
(Oct.–Mar.)
Admission: Adults, $3.00; Children and Students, $2.00

One of Philadelphia's most famous landmarks commemorates an event that has never been proven: that Betsy Ross sewed the first American flag on this spot. Also known as the American Flag House and Betsy Ross Memorial, this modest brick dwelling, just a short walk from the Liberty Bell, probably was the site of Betsy's historic meeting with the "Committee of Three" — George Washington, George Ross, and Robert Morris — in late May or early June of 1776 when they asked her to sew the first flag for the nation. Restored in 1937, the house is typical of those occupied by shopkeepers and craftspeople in the late eighteenth century. Fans of Betsy Ross should also visit the Free Quaker Meeting House (see below), where Betsy was an influential congregant.

Highlights:
A display of historic American flags
A display of tools and fabrics used by eighteenth-century upholsterers
Commercial products that bear Betsy Ross' image

Bishop White House

309 Walnut Street (Map No. 1)

215-965-2305

www.nps.gov/inde/bishop-white.html

Open: Daily; Ranger tours only

Admission: Adults, $2.00; Children, Free. Tickets are obtained at the visitor center (corner of 6th & Market Streets) for a combined one-hour tour with the Todd House (see below).

A visit to the Bishop White House, an elegant three-story Georgian row house, provides a fascinating snapshot of Philadelphia history during the colonial and Revolutionary periods. Not only was the Bishop a recognized patriot leader, brother-in-law to financier Robert Morris, Chaplain of the Second Continental Congress, and host to such luminaries as John Adams, Ben Franklin, and Thomas Jefferson, he was also a personage of great reputation among the "lower sort"—he kept no slaves and hired all his servants, and he was one of the few who stayed in Philadelphia to minister to the sick during the yellow fever epidemics of the 1790s. The house is interpreted as Bishop White would have known it and presents for the visitor a very cohesive sense of how furniture, books, and household items would have been arranged.

Highlights:
One of the first houses to have an indoor "necessary"

Carpenters' Hall

320 Chestnut Street (Map No. 1)
215-925-0167
www.nps.gov/inde/carpenters-hall.html

Open: Tu–Su, 10:00 AM–4:00 PM (Mar.–Dec.); W–Su, 10:00 AM–4:00 PM (Jan.–Feb.)
Admission: Free

It is almost impossible to calculate the contributions that the Carpenters' Company of the City and County of Philadelphia, the oldest trade guild in the country, made to the colonial city and to the architectural history of our country. Comprised of architects, contractors, and engineers, this trade guild built much of colonial Philadelphia, including Independence Hall and their own offices, Carpenters' Hall. The latter probably has played host to more historic meetings, events, and services per square inch than any other colonial building in the country. A partial list would include the First Continental Congress, the establishment of the Secretary of War, the First Bank of the United States, and the first lending library in the United States, the brainchild of Benjamin Franklin. The 1770 Georgian structure is still owned by the Carpenters' Company.

Highlights:
Eighteenth-century carpenter's tools
Five Windsor chairs used by the Continental Congress
Banners carried to celebrate the ratification of the Constitution and the centennial of George Washington's birth

Cedar Grove

Lansdowne Avenue, Fairmount Park West (Map No. 2)
215-684-7922
www.philamuseum.org/collections/parkhouse/cedargrove.shtml

Open: Tu–Su, 10:00 AM–5:00 PM
Admission: $3.00

Administered by the Philadelphia Museum of Art, Cedar Grove actually began life as a small mid-eighteenth-century summer house located near Frankfort, in northeast Philadelphia. The house was expanded in the late eighteenth century and continued to serve five generations of the same family until becoming surrounded by the growing Philadelphia metropolis. In the 1920s, the residence was relocated, stone by stone, to Fairmount Park to serve as a museum. The importance of Cedar Grove lies in its collection of important furniture and household artifacts that have remained in their original context, a rare and fascinating showcase of eighteenth-century domestic life.

Highlights:
An innovative bake oven in the kitchen
A two-sided wall of closets on the second floor
A collection of early Pennsylvania furniture

Charles L. Blockson Afro-American Collection

Temple University (Map No. 2)
Sullivan Hall, First Floor
215-204-6632
www.library.temple.edu/blockson
Open: M–F, 9:00 AM–5:00 PM
Admission: Free

While this collection is technically in the form of a research library, the facility maintains a small exhibition area open to the public. The exhibits change themes periodically to showcase the rich nature of this collection, started by the local historian and author Charles L. Blockson, that illuminates the history and culture of those of African descent.

Highlights:
First editions of Phyllis Wheatley and W. E. B. DuBois
A collection of photos of Negro League players
An edition of Corippus' *Africani Grammatici* (1581)

Chemical Heritage Foundation

315 Chestnut Street (Map No. 1)
215-925-2222
www.chemheritage.org/exhibits/exhibits.html

Open: M–F, 10:00 AM–4:00 PM
Admission: Free

Soon to form the core of the Roy Eddleman Research Museum, the collection at the Chemical Heritage is presently displayed in interim galleries. The collection represents the material culture of the chemical and molecular sciences in addition to an impressive group of seventeenth- to nineteenth-century paintings and sketches of alchemists and alchemy.

Highlights:
Some of the first nylon stockings
N. C. Wyeth's *The Alchemist*
More that 100 early chemical instruments

CIGNA Museum & Art Collection

Two Liberty Place, 1601 Chestnut Street (Map No. 1)

215-761-4907

Open: M–F, 9:00 AM–5:00 PM; Please call for an appointment

Admission: Free

In 1792 a group of prominent Philadelphians founded the
Insurance Company of North America (INA), the first marine
insurance company in the country. After two years of success,
the company broadened their coverage to life insurance — particularly for sea captains facing Barbary Pirates — and fire policies.
In 1982 INA joined Connecticut General Corporation to form
CIGNA. The multinational company has a history of supporting the arts and preserves a distinguished collection of American
art, ranging from the colonial period to contemporary painters, as
well as firefighting memorabilia.

Highlights:

A series of nineteenth-century portraits of Benjamin Franklin
painted on side panels of firefighting wagons

Important watercolors by American artists, including Winslow
Homer, Maurice Prendergast, Charles Demuth, Reginald
Marsh, and Nancy Graves

City Hall

1400 John F. Kennedy Boulevard (Broad & Market Streets, Map No. 1)
215-686-1776

Open: M–F, 9:30 AM–4:15 PM
Admission: Free

The "cathedral" of Philadelphia, City Hall is the most distinctive building in all of downtown. Built on a location set aside by William Penn as the exact geographical center of his plan for Philadelphia, the 548-foot-tall Second Empire–style architectural gem (constructed between 1871 and 1901) is the largest municipal building in the country. Crowned with a cast-iron 37-foot-tall statue of Penn, the largest single piece of sculpture on any building in the world, City Hall is also noteworthy for the more than 250 marble allegorical carvings of animal and human figures created by the famed sculptor Alexander Calder. Representing all the continents, peoples, and governments of the world, these sculptural reliefs are so well integrated into the exterior architecture that thousands pass by daily without noticing them. Fine regional art is displayed year round in special cases on the second and fourth floors. Don't miss the chance to see the panoramic view of the city from the observation deck at the foot of William Penn's statue. The tour office is just inside the east portal.

Highlights:
Sculpture representing the history of Philadelphia and Pennsylvania at the north entrance
The Mayor's Reception Room

The Civil War Library and Museum

1805 Pine Street (Map No. 1)
215-735-8196
www.netreach.net/~cwlm

Open: Th–Sa, 11:00 AM–4:30 PM
Admission: Adults, $5.00; Seniors, $4.00; Students, $3.00; Children 3–12, $2.00

The oldest chartered Civil War institution in America, the Civil War Library and Museum opened in 1888 and contains three floors of unique artifacts and exhibits illuminating this major conflict. The museum, like the Grand Army of the Republic Museum (see below), should not be missed by any Civil War or military history buff. Founded by veteran Union Army, Navy, and Marine Corps officers, the museum's collection is mostly Union related and includes important donations from major figures, such as Ulysses S. Grant, Rutherford B. Hayes, and George Meade. The museum covers all branches of the military, technology of the period, and those who served, including iron-clad warships, cavalry regiments, and African American soldiers. The library is one of the most comprehensive on the Civil War in the country.

Highlights:
A room dedicated to Abraham Lincoln, with an original "wanted" poster for the Lincoln assassination conspirators and life masks of the President.
The stuffed head of Meade's war horse "Old Baldy"
Dress uniforms of both Generals Grant and Meade
Rare weapons, soldier's equipment, and uniforms

Cliveden of the National Trust

6401 Germantown Avenue (Map No. 3)
215-848-1777
www.cliveden.org

Open: Th–Su, noon–4:00 PM (Apr.–Dec.)
Admission: Adults, $8.00 ($7.00 for groups of ten or more); Students, $6.00; Children under 6, Free

Not only has Cliveden survived the wear and tear of more than 240 years, it has also survived being the site of a revolutionary war battle. This circa-1763 stone Middle-Georgian country house of Benjamin Chew, colonial Chief Justice of Pennsylvania, was the refuge of a company of British soldiers during the Battle of Germantown, a pivotal action in which George Washington planned to take back the city of Philadelphia from the British. The battle is reenacted every October. The house remained the chief residency of the Chew family for the most part of two centuries. In addition to its rich historical associations, Cliveden is a premier example of Georgian architectural style. The house is finely decorated with important examples of colonial Philadelphia furniture and paintings, most descending from the Chew family. It is easy to see why Cliveden is considered to be among the finest house museums in America.

Highlights:
A screen of columns that separates the main hall from adjacent rooms
Five large urns on the roof arranged in Palladian fashion
Holes from musket fire still visible in the walls
Thomas Affleck sofa and armchair

Concord School House

6309 Germantown Avenue (Map No. 3)
215-438-2799
www.ushistory.org/germantown/upper/concord.htm

Open: Please call in advance for an appointment
Admission: Free

A genuine one-room schoolhouse, the Concord School House
was built in 1775 for boys and girls of the citizens of
Germantown whose families could afford the tuition. (In 1797
tuition cost $1.50 for a quarter. By 1815 it was $2.00 per quarter.)
In 1818 a second floor was added as a town meeting room. The
building has been maintained meticulously so that visitors can
have a good sense of what is was like to go to school more than
200 years ago, when students were required to bring their own
candles.

Highlights:
Original desks and books
A belfry with a bell
A dunce stool and cap

Declaration (Graff) House

7th & Market Streets (Map No. 1)
215-965-2305
www.nps.gov/inde/declaration-house.html

Open: Daily, 9:00 AM–5:00 PM
Admission: Free

The original Graff house was torn down in 1883 but was rebuilt in 1975 using period plans, vintage photographs, and authentic materials to recreate the house where Thomas Jefferson penned the Declaration of Independence. Thomas Jefferson rented rooms in the brick house in 1776, which at that time was located on the outskirts of town, surrounded by fields, not at this present site. The two second-floor rooms that Jefferson rented—a bedroom and a sitting room—are decorated with period furniture, some reproduction, so that one can marvel under what conditions one of the greatest documents in American history was written in less than three weeks.

Deshler-Morris House

5442 Germantown Avenue (Map No. 3)
215-596-1748
www.nps.gov/edal/dmhouse.htm

Open: F–Su, 1:00 PM–4:00 PM (Apr.–Dec.)
Admission: Free

Built in 1772 as a summer house for Quaker merchant David
Deshler, this stone mansion has the distinction of playing host to
two major figures on opposite sides of the American Revolution.
Originally built as a four-room cottage, its nine-room addition
made it one of the most elegant homes in the region. British
General Sir William Howe conscripted it as his headquarters
during the Battle of Germantown in October 1777. Most importantly, though, it is the oldest surviving presidential residence in
the nation, nicknamed the "Germantown White House" after
President Washington lived here during the yellow fever epidemic of 1793. It is this residency that is highlighted in today's interpretation, giving visitors a glimpse into the private world of the
nation's first President.

Highlights:
A red sofa belonging to Washington
A Washington family portrait that includes the enslaved servant
Willie Lee
A dining room where Washington held Cabinet meetings

Drexel University Museums

Drexel Collection, Westphal Picture Gallery, Paul Peck Alumni Center

3141 Chestnut Street; 32nd & Market Streets (Map No. 2)

215-895-0480

www.drexel.edu/drexelcollection

Open: M–F, 9:00 AM–5:00 PM; 3:30 PM–5:00 PM (Picture Gallery)

Admission: Free

When financier Anthony J. Drexel died in 1893, he left behind not only a legacy on Wall Street but a university in his name. Part of the original main building on campus was designed to showcase artwork for the edification and delight of students and faculty. The Drexel Collection consists of paintings, furniture, and decorative arts, mostly from the eighteenth and nineteenth centuries. The third floor of the main building houses The Antoinette and Ray Westphal Picture Gallery. The gallery has been restored to its original style, complete with striking red cloth on the walls as background to the artwork. There is now an additional gallery in the Paul Peck Alumni Center, a recently refurbished Frank Furness building originally built for the 1876 Centennial. Drexel University will continue to expand its museum space, but the university is on the leading edge of virtual museum creation for some of its holdings, starting with the Historic Costume Collection, part of the Drexel Digital Museum Project, at http://digimuse.cis.drexel.edu/.

Highlights:
A Regency chess table (c. 1815) built for Napoleon Bonaparte
A David Rittenhouse tall-case clock (c. 1774)
The Shepherd by Jean-Baptiste Camille Corot

The Eakins Gallery at Thomas Jefferson University

Jefferson Alumni Hall, 1020 Locust Street (Map No. 1)

215-955-7947

www.tju.edu/eakins

Open: M–Sa, 10:00 AM–4:00 PM

Admission: Free; Request access at the security desk

One of Thomas Eakins' most famous paintings is *The Gross Clinic* (1875), offering an unflinching view of a surgeon in the midst of a procedure in the operating theater of Jefferson Medical College. Eakins' relationship with the College, now Thomas Jefferson University, was long and mutually profitable. Believing that anatomy was crucial to his craft of painting, he studied the subject twice at Jefferson and painted many portraits of the faculty, of which Dr. Samuel Gross' is just one fine example. The study paid off, as Eakins is widely considered to be the finest American realist painter of the nineteenth century. Other paintings by him, and a portion of the University's collection of over 300 works, can be seen in the gallery.

Highlights:

Portrait of a Soldier (1917) by Susan Macdowell Eakins (Ms. Thomas Eakins)

Athena/Minerva, a second-century Roman marble sculpture

A display of early medical equipment

East Africa Resource Center

3809 Pearl Street (Map No. 2)
215-382-3191
www.eastafricacenter.net

Open: F & Sa, 11:00 AM–7:00 PM
Admission: Free

The East Africa Resource Center is a unique, comprehensive exhibition of artifacts relating to the nomadic tribes of Ethiopia, Somalia, Eritrea, Sudan, Uganda, Kenya, and Tanzania. The collection includes a complete nomadic shelter, photographs, sculpture, textiles, pottery, and textual material. Given the social and environmental pressures on these groups, the material preserved at the center has become an important resource for information about the history of these tribes. Like many other museums in this book, the center has a vibrant public outreach program, hosting classes, performances, and films on East African culture.

Eastern State Penitentiary Historic Site

2124 Fairmount Avenue (Map No. 2)
215-236-3300
www.easternstate.org

Open: W–Su, 10:00 AM–5:00 PM (Apr.–Nov.); Last entry, 4:00 PM
Admission: Adults, $7.00; Students and Seniors, $5.00; Children 7–12, $3.00. Group rates are available.
Important Note: Children under 7 not permitted on the site.

The massive Eastern State Penitentiary in the Fairmount section of Philadelphia, once the most expensive building in America and now a National Historic Landmark, is remarkable for its innovative architecture and its experimental attempt to reform prisoners though severe isolation. Built in 1829, its revolutionary radial design featured lines of individual cells, like wheel spokes emanating from the central guard quarters. It was in each of these 8-by-12-foot cells that convicted criminals lived out their sentences, forbidden to read, write, sing, meet, or communicate with other inmates or even exercise more than an hour a day in their individual yards. Called "maniac-making" by the *London Times*, the jail remained in operation until the early 1970s, with some of the restrictions lifted over the years. It fell into disrepair until finally bought by the city, renovated, and opened as a museum. Eastern State Penitentiary was held as a model of idealism in penal reform and a model of prison architecture, and its design can be found in hundreds of prisons throughout the world.

Highlights:
A central observation rotunda
The solitary confinement yards

Ebenezer Maxwell Mansion

200 W. Tulpehocken Street (Map No. 3)
215-438-1861
www.maxwellmansion.org

Open: F–Su, 1:00 PM–4:00 PM
Admission: Adults, $5.00; Students and Children under 12, $4.00

A splendid example of the enthusiasm of Victorian domestic design, and a must see for those interested in Victorian taste and architecture, no surface in the Ebenezer Maxwell house is undecorated or unadorned: faux finishes, elaborate plaster carvings and woodwork, and hand-painted ceilings all attest to the easy availability of material goods to the rising middle class of the era. Built by cloth merchant Ebenezer Maxwell in 1859, this stone mansion is a wonderful lesson in an important era of American social history.

Highlights:
Modern conveniences in the kitchen, including an apple corer and bean slicer
Extensively landscaped gardens
An important collection of children's toys in the nursery, including an original Milton Bradley set of checkers

Edgar Allan Poe National Historic Site

532 N. 7th Street (Map No. 1)
215-597-8780
www.nps.gov/edal/

Open: W–Su, 9:00 AM–5:00 PM
Admission: Free

"As my worldly circumstances were somewhat less embarrassed than his own, I was permitted to be at the expense of renting, and furnishing in a style which suited the rather fantastic gloom of our common temper, a time-eaten and grotesque mansion." Perhaps Edgar Allan Poe was writing from experience when he penned this description in *Murders of the Rue Morgue* in 1841, as Philadelphia was home to this gothic master from 1838 to 1844 during his most prolific period when some of his greatest stories and poems were written, including *The Fall of the House of Usher*, *The Pit and the Pendulum*, and *The Masque of the Red Death*. The National Park Service now administers this three-building complex that features the only remaining of several apartments rented by Poe for himself, his wife, and his mother-in-law. Some scholars suggest that his most famous poem, *The Raven*, was begun in these very rooms. The site is nearly bare as nothing remains of Poe's belongings or furniture, but the austerity of the original walls, floors, and fireplaces provide a fitting atmosphere to reflect on one of America's most important writers. There is an exhibit of Poe's life and work, and an audiovisual presentation places the site in context.

The Edwin and Trudy Weaver Historical Dental Museum

Temple University (Map No. 2)

3223 N. Broad Street, Third Floor

215-707-2816

http://www.temple.edu/dentistry/museum.htm

Open: M–F, 9:00 AM–5:00 PM; Please call for tours

Admission: Free

At its founding in 1863, the Philadelphia Dental College began collecting artifacts of the trade. The collection, now located at the Temple University School of Dentistry, continues to expand and is home to more items than the National Dental Museum itself. The museum offers a fascinating look at the origins and history of dentistry in America, from colonial times to today, including an array of early instruments such as the "scarificator," which was used to bleed patients, a bucket of teeth that were the legacy of "Painless Parker," who reportedly pulled 357 teeth in one day, early x-ray and casting machines, and a selection of drills.

Highlights:

The first dental chair used in America

Dental instruments with mother-of-pearl handles made by Paul Revere

A recreation of a pre-electric Victorian dental office, complete with foot-pedal drill

Elfreth's Alley Museum

126 Elfreth's Alley (Map No. 1)

215-574-0560

www.elfrethsalley.org

Open: M–Sa, 10:00 AM–5:00 PM; Su, noon–5:00 PM (Mar.–Oct.);
Th–Sa, 10:00 AM–5:00 PM; Su, noon–5:00 PM (Nov.–Feb.)

Admission: Adults, $2.00; Children 6–18, $1.00; Children under 6, Free.
Free for everyone on July 4.

Named for the mid-eighteenth-century blacksmith who owned most of the houses and rented them to fellow artisans, the 33 houses of Elfreth's Alley comprise the oldest continuously inhabited street in the United States, with the oldest surviving house dating back to 1720. This is an opportunity to experience as best we can the flavor and scale of an authentic colonial residential street. Anyone who wants to really step back in time has to make a visit to this fascinating street. While most of these modest Georgian and Federal style buildings are still privately owned (and visitors should keep this in mind), two are open to the public: No. 124, the former residence of a chair maker, and No. 126, once owned by a woman needleworker, which has been converted into a museum dedicated to the history of colonial life. Here visitors can learn about period architecture, including the layout of the distinctive Trinity construction, furnishings that would be typical for craftspeople of the time, and the story of how this street was able to survive essentially intact for more than 300 years and counting.

Fabric Workshop and Museum

1315 Cherry Street, 5th Floor (Map No. 1)
215-568-1111
www.fabricworkshop.org

Open: M–F, 10:00 AM–6:00 PM; Sa, noon–4:00 PM
Admission: Free

Housed in an old industrial building, the Fabric Workshop is the
only museum in the United States dedicated to artists working in
textiles and other similar experimental materials. The museum
has been a significant patron of artists and consists of three exhibition galleries as well as 12,500 square feet of construction and
print studios that are open to the public, offering visitors the
ability to see contemporary works in progress. The permanent
collection features works by artists such as Louise Bourgeois and
Robert Venturi. Exhibits are changed frequently to showcase the
wealth of current and collected material

Fairmount Waterworks Interpretive Center

640 Waterworks Drive (Map No. 2)

215-685-4908

www.fairmountwaterworks.org

Open: Tu–Sa, 10:00 AM–5:00 PM; Su, 1:00 PM–5:00 PM

Admission: Free

The Interpretive Center is a fascinating mix of old and new: statuesque neoclassical buildings house technologically cutting-edge interactive exhibits. The late-eighteenth-century yellow fever epidemics heightened Philadelphia's awareness of the necessity of clean drinking water, and Philadelphia became the first major American city to regard the delivery of safe water as a municipal responsibility. Built on the banks of the Schuylkill between 1819 and 1822, the picturesque Waterworks were actually an efficient series of pumps to raise water from the river into reservoirs. Even then the complex was considered a tourist attraction, with the Engine House remodeled in 1835 as a restaurant to serve the thousands of visitors it attracted. Now a National Historic Landmark, the facility has been retrofitted by the Philadelphia Water Department to become an interpretive center to educate visitors on the historic need for water and the current necessity of protecting the Earth's limited water resources.

Highlights:

A simulated helicopter flight from the Delaware Bay to the headwaters of the Delaware or Schuylkill rivers

A working model of the Fairmount Water Works

River balconies and promenade

Federal Reserve Bank of Philadelphia "Money in Motion"

6th & Arch Streets (Map No. 1)

215-574-6000

www.phil.frb.org/money_in_motion/index.html

Open: M–F, 9:30 AM–4:30 PM; Sa & Su, 10:00 AM–4:00 PM

Admission: Free

It is fitting that this museum, dedicated to telling the story of central banking, is in the city where American banking was born. The exhibits at the Federal Reserve Bank trace the history of the national banking system from pre-Revolutionary times to the world after September 11, 2001. Visitors can learn about how money is made and how savings are kept secure while displays include a station that lets you pit your wits against counterfeiters and an explanation of the mysteries of the Federal Reserve Board.

Highlights:

A coin and currency collection, from the sixteenth century to the present

A 25-foot tower of shredded money totaling $100 million

Fireman's Hall

147 N. Second Street (Map No. 1)
215-923-1438
www.mfrconsultants.com/pfd/museum.shtml

Open: Tu–Sa, 10:00 AM–5:00 PM; first Friday of each month, –9:00 PM
Admission: Free

It seems only appropriate that this museum dedicated to the history of firefighting should be in Philadelphia, as Benjamin Franklin organized the country's first volunteer fire company here in 1736. The museum is a favorite of children with its collection of fire trucks, animated displays of bucket brigades, firemen's living quarters, and even a display dedicated to the role and importance of the fire horse. Fireman's Hall is a restored firehouse built in 1876.

Highlights:
A hand pump said to be used by Ben Franklin himself
A brass firemen's pole that goes from the third to the first floor
An apparatus room featuring hand pumpers and steamers, where touching is encouraged

Fort Mifflin

Fort Mifflin Road (Map No. 2)

215-685-4167

www.phila.gov/recreation/historical/fortmifflin.html

Open: W–Su, 10:00 AM–4:00 PM (Apr.–Nov.)

Admission: Adults, $5.00; Seniors, $4.50; Students, $4.00; Children 3–12, $2.00. Call for group rates.

The British began construction of this fort on an island in the Delaware River in 1772. Left incomplete, the fort was occupied by General Thomas Mifflin and several hundred continentals in the fall of 1777 after Washington's defeat at the Battle of Brandywine allowed General William Howe and 20,000 troops to occupy Philadelphia. The British depended on supplies brought into the city by ships, which were vulnerable to guns in the fort. The continental troops endured heavy barrages but finally succumbed to an amphibious assault in November 1777. But the fort had held out just long enough for winter weather to set in and keep the British from pursuing Washington and his troops at Valley Forge, thus allowing the continentals time to regroup and continue the war to its successful conclusion. This national monument and historic landmark has been restored to its 1834 appearance and offers buildings, rooms, and casements for visitors to explore. Gun and cannon demonstrations and military reenactments are a regular feature of the site, so it is well-worth calling ahead for a schedule of events.

Highlights:

"Bombproof" casements used to shelter troops under attack

Restored dungeons

Franklin Court

314-322 Market Street (Map No. 1)
215-965-2305
www.nps.gov/inde/franklin-court.html

Open: Daily, 10:00 AM–5:00 PM (Post office opens at 9:00 AM)
Admission: Free

As befitting such a complex character, the city's museum dedicated to Benjamin Franklin is actually a series of interesting and
specialized installations. This printer, diplomat, inventor, scientist,
revolutionary, author, fireman, postmaster, and librarian, to name
just a few of his avocations, has such a hold on the popular imagination, it seems only reasonable that he have a multitude of
museums paying him homage. While Franklin was not a native
son (he came to Philadelphia from Boston at age 17),
Philadelphia has embraced this fascinating Founding Father as
the patron saint of the city. Just a flip through this book will
show the reader the breadth of Franklin's interests and influence.

Franklin Court

Franklin's house, the only one he actually owned, stood inside
this court until it was razed in 1812. In its place is famed architect
Robert Venturi's "Ghost Structure," a towering skeleton that
recreates the profile of the original three-story, ten-room brick
house. Visitors can look through portals to see the original privy
pits, wells, and foundation. Engraved on stones outside are witty
sections of his letters relating to the building of the house in the
early 1760s, when he was the Continental emissary to England
and France. Franklin spent most of the next 20 years abroad, so
he was not often at the house. He returned in 1785 and lived here

until he died in 1790. Thomas Jefferson was among the last persons to visit him at his home.

Underground Museum

Highlighting Franklin's multifaceted career and accomplishments, the Underground Museum features examples of his many inventions, including a swim fin, bifocals, his famous stove, lightning rods, and even a glass armonica, a set of graduated glass bowls on a rotating shaft that produce tones when a finger is pressed to their rims. Wolfgang Mozart was so intrigued by this instrument that he composed music especially for it. The museum also presents animated dioramas illustrating pivotal moments in Franklin's diplomatic career, including the response to the Stamp Act, the Court of Versailles, where Franklin was trying to encourage the French to aid the Americans, and the Constitutional Congress of 1787.

United States Postal Service Museum and Post Office

Along with all his other interests, Benjamin Franklin was also one of the first Postmaster Generals of the United States. Since there was no American flag in 1775 when this office was opened at 314-316 Market Street, it remains the only post office in the United States that does not fly a flag. Postal employees still hand stamp "B. Free Franklin" to cancel mail. The museum contains such curiosities as a Pony Express mail pouch and original copies of Franklin's *Pennsylvania Gazette* as well as rare and unusual stamps.

318 Market Street

Built by Franklin during the 1780s to take advantage of the higher rents he could command as a result of the city's booming economy, this house museum is unusual in that it is a graphic exhibit in architectural archaeology and the history of building. "Fragments of Franklin's Court" allows visitors to experience the life cycle of this house from Franklin's original design and specifications, to changes made in the nineteenth century, to the detailed detective work that was done to prove where architectural elements like fireplaces, doorways, and stairwells once stood. Placed throughout the house are furnishings and interior detailing to show how the house would have been furnished and decorated in Franklin's time.

Printing Office and Bindery

Benjamin Franklin was originally trained as a printer, apprenticing at his elder brother's shop in Boston. When he was promoted to the status of master printer in Philadelphia, he took over the management of *The Pennsylvania Gazette*, which became the most successful newspaper in the colonies, the first American paper to be sent out colony-wide. But Benjamin Franklin was not just a printer of books; he was the writer, editor, and printer of many broadsides, pamphlets, and almanacs. The park service has recreated an eighteenth-century print shop here at 320 Market Street, with demonstrations of the printing and binding equipment done by park rangers in colonial costume.

General Advertiser

At 322 Market Street is the restored office of *The General Advertiser*, the newspaper published by Benjamin Franklin Bache, the grandson of Benjamin Franklin. The site was actually the former residence of James Wilson, editor of *The Aurora* and grandfather to Woodrow, the 28th President of the United States.

The Franklin Institute

220 N. 20th Street (Map No. 1)

215-448-1200

www.fi.edu

Open: Daily, 9:30 AM–5:00 PM; F & Sa, –9:00 PM (Mandell Center)

Admission: Adults, $12.75 (base admission); Children and Seniors, $10.00

The Franklin Institute is among the world's most important science museums. Its current building was erected in 1934 and encompasses an entire city block, but the museum actually has a history going back to 1824, when it opened an exhibit in Independence Hall to honor the scientific achievements of Benjamin Franklin. The collections of this institution are truly staggering: original Franklin lightning rods, an Edison light bulb, the Wright brother's wind tunnel and flight notebooks, steam-powered bicycles, an eighteenth-century automaton, early Kodak cameras, an actual lunar module, Muybridge's Animal Locomotion series, and a Baldwin locomotive, to name just a fraction of this interesting and unique collection. It is the interactive nature of the displays, however, that make the museum world renowned. Innovative and imaginative, they make learning about science and technology fun for everyone. This is a museum where toddlers to high school students can spend hours engaged in all sorts of activities that help explain scientific concepts. The gigantic walk-though model heart, recently renovated, has been a highlight for children and adults for decades and shouldn't be missed. One of the most popular exhibits is the Franklin Air Show that features the history and mechanics of flight and includes a great flight simulator and real aircraft, such as an original Wright B Flyer. Another excellent exhibit is the Sports Challenge where children and adults can enjoy lots of activities related to the science of sports, such as seeing how fast you can really throw a baseball or football as measured by a radar gun, test your reaction time while sitting in simulated drag racers, measure your vertical jump on a special machine, and see how far you can fly in a ski-jump simulator. The Institute also houses the excellent Fels Planetarium and the Tuttleman Imax Theater in the Mandell Center; both require separate ticketing. You simply can't go wrong with this fascinating and innovative museum.

Highlights:
The gigantic life-like model heart that you can walk through
A world-class planetarium
A Lunar Module and Lunar Rover
A major exhibit on the history of electricity

Free Library of Philadelphia Rare Book Department

1901 Vine Street (Map No. 1)
215-686-5416
www.library.phila.gov
Open: M–F, tours at 11:00 AM, or by appointment
Admission: Free

Housed in a room reassembled from its original location and named for the benefactor William McIntire Elkins, the rare book department at the Free Library is a bibliophile's dream. The collection ranges from 4,000-year-old Sumerian cuneiform tablets, Beatrix Potter illustrations, and illuminated medieval manuscripts to early American children's books and German Frakturs. Tours highlight the strengths of the collection, while the exhibit cabinets change three to four times a year to showcase the depth of a particular topic.

Free Quaker Meeting House

5th & Arch Streets (Map No. 1)
215-629-5801
www.historicphiladelphia.org

Open: Please call for visiting hours
Admission: Please call for admission information

The events surrounding the British colonies' secession from Great Britain so stirred a group of Quakers that they took up arms against the Crown, even knowing that this action would have them "read out," or expelled from the pacifist group. A splinter group of approximately 200, calling themselves Free Quakers, started their own meeting house in 1783. Once the new nation was established, the distinction was no longer necessary, and over the years participation waned. Betsy Ross, one of the last two congregants, helped lock the doors in 1834 when she was 82. The brick building is notable for its nationalist architectural influences on the traditional plain Quaker style. Used variously as a school, a library, and then a plumbing warehouse, the structure has been restored to its 1784 appearance and now houses offices for Historic Philadelphia, Inc., in addition to operating as a museum.

Highlights:
An exhibit on Betsy Ross' flag design, including the original five-pointed star tissue pattern
Original benches and an original window

Gazela of Philadelphia

Penn's Landing at Columbus Boulevard & Market Street (Map No. 1)
215-238-0280
www.gazela.org

Open: Sa & Su, 10:00 AM–5:00 PM (When in port)
Admission: Free

If you are a lover of wooden ships and sailing, you will want to take time to visit the *Gazela* berthed just south of the Independence Seaport Museum (see below). Owned and maintained by the Philadelphia Ship Preservation Guild, the barkentine *Gazela* is one of the world's oldest operational tall ships. Built in 1901, the *Gazela* operated for 70 years carrying fisherman from Portugal to Newfoundland's Grand Banks until she was purchased to be shown as a historic wooden vessel. Since becoming an educational exhibit, the *Gazela* has been part of many tall-ship gatherings up and down the East Coast. Docked alongside the *Gazela* is the tugboat *Jupiter*, which was launched in 1902 and is one of the oldest operational tugboats in existence. Please call or visit the ship's Web site to see when she is in port.

Germantown Historical Society

5501 Germantown Avenue (Map No. 3)
215-844-0514
www.germantownhistory.org

Open: Tu & Th, 9:00 AM–5:00 PM; Su, 1:00 PM–5:00 PM
Admission: Adults, $5.00; Seniors and Students, $4.00; Children, $2.00

The first German settlement in the new world, Germantown was founded in 1683 by immigrants from the Rhine Valley in response to an advertisement placed by William Penn. Now part of urban Philadelphia, the area is still proudly distinct and has played various roles in Philadelphia history, as the site of the Battle of Germantown, as one of the first urban villages, where a melting-pot population created a group identity, as a suburb for the working and middle classes during the Industrial Revolution, and as the nation's first commuter suburb served by one of the nation's first railroads. The Germantown Historical Society has an astounding number of artifacts in their collection, ranging from seventeenth-century furniture to a costume collection second only to that of the Philadelphia Museum of Art. Their textile collection is also extremely important. In fact, the holdings are so large that it is common for visitors to make special arrangements to see collections and artifacts that are not currently on display. If you are visiting Philadelphia and are interested in eighteenth-century material culture, whether textiles, costumes, furniture, or everyday household items, it would be well worth calling the Germantown Historical Society to receive a "behind-the-scenes" tour, possibly a high point of your visit.

Glen Foerd

5001 Grant Avenue (Map No. 2)
215-632-5330
www.glenfoerd.org

Open: Tu–F, 10:00 AM–2:00 PM. Please call two days in advance for guided entrance.
Admission: $5.00

Built as Glengarry by presidential adviser Charles Macalaster in 1853, its name was changed to Glen Foerd by its second owner, Robert Foerdere, in 1893. It was Foerdere who renovated the Italianate summer home into an Edwardian country house, enlarging it to the 25-room mansion that we know today. The architectural elegance of the creamy stone mansion with airy wraparound porch is paralleled in the marvelous collection of antique furniture, rare books, and ornamental plaster inside. Glen Foerd's impressive picture gallery, inspired by the Tate in London, contains numerous important works of art, including paintings by Rembrandt, Constable, Van Gogh, and Monet. Visitors can also walk the beautiful grounds, which are interesting both for the variety of trees and flower plantings and the ancillary buildings and facilities attached to the estate.

Highlights:
A Haskel player pipe organ
A formal rose garden in the 18-acre grounds

Grand Army of the Republic Museum

4278 Griscom Street (Map No. 2)

215-289-6484

http://garmuslib.org

Open: Tu, noon–4:00 PM; W, 10:00 AM–2:00 PM; first Sunday of each month, noon–5:00 PM. Please call ahead before visiting.

Admission: Free (Donation suggested)

Begun by a chapter of Civil War veterans, this museum is tucked away in the Northeast's Frankford neighborhood in a three-story brick building built in 1796. The collection is the delight of any Civil War history buff, as there is a huge array of artifacts, personal memorabilia, documents, photographs, battle relics, and paintings to view, including a strip of pillowcase from Lincoln's deathbed, 6th Pennsylvania cavalry lances, and a post from the stockade of the notorious Andersonville Prison. There are also rifles, swords, and shells on display. All of these add up to a sobering lesson on the impact that this war had on the nation's identity. At the Sunday open houses, costumed docents welcome visitors.

Highlights:

Tree trunks from the Battle of Chickamauga imbedded with cannon balls

Handcuffs found in John Wilkes Booth's suitcase, intended for Lincoln's kidnap

Original *Harper's Weekly* and *Philadelphia Inquirer* newspapers for the entire war

Grumblethorpe

5267 Germantown Avenue (Map No. 3)

215-843-4820

www.philalandmarks.org/page_houses/grumble/home/

Open: Tu, Th, & Su, noon–4:00 PM (Mar. 15–Dec. 1)

Admission: Adults, $4.00; Seniors, Students, and Individuals in groups of ten or more (groups by appointment), $2.00

Built in 1744 as a summer house by Quaker wine importer John Wister, Grumblethorpe was held by the same family until the 1950s, when the house became a museum. This stone-and-oak Pennsylvania German house witnessed national history—British General James Agnew died here from wounds received during the Battle of Germantown—and holds more than 150 years worth of family treasures, giving a vivid glimpse of the domestic life of earlier periods. The Wister family itself produced several singular personalities. Owen Wister, the author of the first Western novel, *The Virginian*, was a cousin and frequent visitor to Grumblethorpe. The grounds, extensively and painstakingly recreated, contain the oldest ginkgo tree in America.

Highlights:

The "courting door" in the parlor, for suitors to talk to the Wister ladies from the street

A chair made by Solomon Fussell, who also made chairs for Independence Hall

Historic Bartram's Garden

54th Street & Lindbergh Boulevard (Map No. 2)

215-729-5281

www.bartramsgarden.org

Open: Grounds, Daily, 10:00 AM–5:00 PM; House tours, Tu–Su, noon–4:00 PM (Mar.–Dec.)

Admission: Adults, $6.00; Seniors, $4.00; Children 12 and under, Free. Inquire for group tours.

It is hard to imagine that a bucolic 45-acre colonial homestead survived for centuries within the bounds of a bustling city. The eighteenth-century protoecologist John Bartram, a Quaker farmer who devoted his life to plant collecting and preserving, built the first botanical garden in America on this spot in 1728, introducing more than 200 native plants into cultivation. Called the "Father of American Botany," this self-taught naturalist became Royal Botanist to George III and with his son William, traveled extensively in the colonies, finding and cataloging plants as far south as Florida. The Bartrams unknowingly saved the Franklinia tree, perhaps their most famous discovery, from extinction, and all existing Franklinias come from the specimens they collected. Bartram House was originally a small Swedish farmhouse that stood on the original property; John Bartram enlarged it and used it as both home and office for his extensive plant-collecting business. Several founding fathers, especially Benjamin Franklin, were frequent visitors here. In 1783, six years after John's death, his family issued the first printed plant catalog in America and supplied plants for Independence Hall, George Washington's Mount Vernon, and Thomas Jefferson's Monticello. In their botanic garden and greenhouses, the

Bartrams eventually propagated more than 4,000 species of native and exotic plants. With great prescience, the railroad magnate Andrew M. Eastwick bought the property in 1850 to save it from encroaching industrialism. There are ongoing restorations, so visitors may be lucky enough to observe an archaeological or preservation project in progress.

Highlights:

The *Franklinia alatamaha* tree, which they named for their friend, Ben

The house with original belongings from both John and William Bartram

An early cider press

Historic Rittenhouse Town

206 Lincoln Drive (Map No. 3)

215-438-5711

www.rittenhousetown.org

Open: Sa & Su, noon–4:00 PM (Jun.–Sept.); By appointment (Oct.–May);
Group tours by appointment at all times

Admission: Adults, $5.00; Seniors and Children, $3.00

Founded by William Rittenhouse in 1690, Historic Rittenhouse
Town, a National Historic Landmark, is the site of America's
first paper mill and treats the curious to a very clear picture of
what life was like for colonial craftsmen and women. When
viewing this village of seven houses maintained as they would
have been in the eighteenth century, a visitor discovers just how
important paper was in the colonial period — the dissemination of
knowledge through letters, newspapers, broadsides, and books
was what united the thirteen colonies in their rebellion. Indeed,
Rittenhouse town itself occupied a strategic location during the
British occupation of Philadelphia. Reports of British behavior
were brought through Rittenhouse town to General
Washington's camp. David Rittenhouse, mathematician,
astronomer, statesman, and first president of the United States
Mint, was born here in 1732. Tours include the William
Rittenhouse Homestead, the 1707 Rittenhouse home, and a
papermaking demonstration.

Highlights:

A working model of an eighteenth-century paper mill

An eighteenth-century bakehouse

An exhibit on food in an early German American community

Historic St. George's United Methodist Church

235 N. 4th Street (Map No. 1)
215-925-7788
www.geocities.com/Athens/Forum/1767/

Open: Daily, 1:00 PM–4:00 PM
Admission: Free

"The Cradle of American Methodism," St. George's, erected in the early 1760s and bought by the Methodists in 1769, is the world's oldest Methodist church in continuous service. Robert Morris, the primary financier of the American Revolution, prayed all night here on New Year's Eve of 1776, asking for guidance in securing money for the Continental Army. In keeping with William Penn's tradition of tolerance, African Americans were allowed to worship at St. George's; however, their services were held separately and at five in the morning. Ultimately, Richard Allen, the first licensed black Methodist preacher, left the church and founded the Mother Bethel AME Church (see below). By the 1920s St. George's congregation had dwindled, and the building was either to be destroyed or moved in favor of the Benjamin Franklin Bridge construction. The church won a legal battle to remain where it is, with the bridge looming just yards from the site. The church was revitalized due to its historic importance and now is both a museum and active place of worship.

Highlights:
John Wesley's handwritten hymnal
The oldest Methodist chalice in the world

Historical Society of Pennsylvania

1300 Locust Street (Map No. 1)
215-732-6200
www.hsp.org
Open: Tu–Th, 12:30 PM–5:30 PM; W, –8:30 PM; F, 10:30 AM–5:30 PM
Admission: $1.00

The Historical Society of Pennsylvania is an important research institute for the history of Philadelphia and the state of Pennsylvania. While the library is the chief attraction for visitors who wish to consult primary sources, the Historical Society regularly showcases selections of printed and written materials drawn from its vast holdings. These exhibits are periodically refreshed and are designed to explore topics of local and regional interest. The Historical Society began its collection in the early nineteenth century, and it has been able to assemble an impressive range of artifacts, including William Penn's archives and Martha Washington's cookbook.

History of Nursing Museum

Old Pine Building, Pennsylvania Hospital (Map No. 1)
8th & Spruce Streets
215-829-3971 ext. 5
www.nursinghistory.org

Open: M–F, 8:00 AM–4:00 PM
Admission: Free

Beginning as a Bicentennial project, the History of Nursing Museum was created in 1974 entirely by donations of memorabilia from nurses and friends of nursing. Since then, the museum has become a repository for nurses all over the country to contribute diaries, letters, books, caps, equipment, and many historical items to allow visitors to appreciate the importance of this career in the nation's and medical history. Be sure to pick up the self-guided tour pamphlet at the hospital's main entrance.

Highlights:
A display of uniforms and badges of honor prior to 1920
Florence Nightingale letters

Independence National Historical Park (Secured Area)

Independence Hall, Congress Hall, Old City Hall, Liberty Bell Center

Between Market & Chestnut Streets and 5th & 6th Streets (Map No. 1)
215-965-2035
www.nps.gov/inde/

Open: Daily, 9:00 AM–5:00 PM

Admission: Free; timed tickets are required for access to Independence Hall (Mar.–Dec.). All visitors must enter through the security screening facilities.

At the heart of "America's Most Historic Square Mile" and the most visited destination in Philadelphia as well as one of the top tourist destinations in the United States, Independence National Historical Park incorporates the buildings used by the founding fathers in their deliberations to break from England, their creation of the world's first democracy, and their administration of the early Republic. The clock tower of Independence Hall and the Liberty Bell are two of the most recognized icons of America. The park is nearly 45 acres of beautiful tree-lined streets (some still paved with stones that were tread by those who signed the Declaration of Independence), and a number of buildings and exhibits are open to the public. Most of the buildings in the park are covered in this book under their own names and are listed at the end of this entry; those at the center of the park are in a secure area and are discussed here. Give yourself plenty of time to wander and soak in the history preserved throughout the park. It is much less commercial and more authentic than most historic preserves in the country.

Liberty Bell Center

Market Street between 5th & 6th Streets
www.nps.gov/inde/liberty-bell.html

Located in a new site on the west side of Independence Mall, the Liberty Bell is now approached through a series of exhibits showcasing how the bell was represented since its inaugural ringing to announce the first public reading of the Declaration of Independence. One display shows x-rays of its famous cracks. The Bell's new glass structure presents an inspirational view of Independence Hall.

Independence Hall Museum

Chestnut Street between 5th & 6th Streets
www.nps.gov/inde/indep-hall.html

America's most historic building was erected between 1732 and 1756 as the Pennsylvania State House. Subsequent events changed the course of history, and its name was changed to Independence Hall. The Second Continental Congress met here in the spring of 1776, united in anger over "the shot heard 'round the world," in Concord, Massachusetts. In the same Assembly Hall the Declaration of Independence was signed, George Washington was appointed Commander-in-Chief of the Continental Army, and the Constitution was adopted. The Great Essentials exhibit upstairs in the west wing displays the Declaration of Independence, the Articles of Confederation, and the Constitution of the United States. Visitors can also admire the graceful silver inkstand that according to tradition was used during the signing of both the Declaration and the Constitution. George Washington's chair is here, with its decoration of a sun on the horizon, which Benjamin Franklin famously decided was rising, not setting for the new nation.

Congress Hall

6th & Chestnut Streets
www.nps.gov/inde/congress-hall.html

To the west of Independence Hall stands Congress Hall, where the newly formed United States House and Senate met when Philadelphia was the capital of the United States from 1790 to 1800. Congress Hall has been restored to the way it looked between 1793 and 1800. In 1793 George Washington was inaugurated here for a second term, and John Adams was sworn into office as our second President four years later before an international audience. The Bill of Rights was ratified here in 1791. The second floor contains the Senate Chamber and is open daily from 3:00 PM to 5:00 PM.

Old City Hall

5th & Chestnut Streets
www.nps.gov/inde/old-city-hall.html

To the east of Independence Hall is the original City Hall of Philadelphia, which was used by the first Supreme Court from 1791 to 1800 until the federal government moved to Washington, D.C. It also housed the nation's first immigration center, as thousands of immigrants went through to gain citizenship in the later part of the eighteenth century.

See also Bishop White House, Carpenters' Hall, Declaration House, Franklin Court, New Hall Military Museum, Second Bank of the United States, Thaddeus Kosciuszko National Memorial, Todd House

Independence Seaport Museum

211 S. Columbus Boulevard & Walnut Street (Map No. 1)

215-925-5439

www.phillyseaport.org

Open: Daily, 10:00 AM–5:00 PM

Admission: Adults, $9.00; Children under 12, $6.00; Seniors, $8. Free admission Sun, 10:00 AM–noon (not applicable to groups)

Dedicated to preserving and sharing the maritime heritage of the Delaware River and Bay, Independence Seaport Museum features an interactive exhibit that explains the physics, design, and construction of water-borne craft and allows visitors to get aboard a 22-foot boat. Other permanent exhibits focus on the China Trade, deep-sea exploration, and the operations of merchant shipping and docks. Throughout, hundreds of artifacts from the museum's extensive collection, including detailed ship models, are on display. Perhaps one of the most compelling reasons to visit the museum is that the ticket price allows you to go aboard the protected cruiser USS *Olympia* and the World War II submarine USS *Becuna*, both National Historic Landmarks. The *Olympia* is noteworthy as the oldest steel warship afloat in the world. Touring this ship alone is reason enough to visit the museum. The museum also offers a ticket option that allows visitors to take a ferry across the Delaware River to the Camden Aquarium and the battleship USS *New Jersey*.

Highlights:

A world-class ship model collection

A three-story replica of the Benjamin Franklin Bridge

A miniature crane that allows visitors to "unload cargo"

Johnson House Historic Site

6306 Germantown Avenue (Map No. 3)

215-438-1768

www.johnsonhouse.org

Open: Th & F, 10:00 AM–4:00 PM (tours by appointment); Sa, 1:00 PM–4:00 PM (tours at 1:30 PM, 2:30 PM, and 3:30 PM)

Admission: Adults, $5.00; Children under 12, $2.00; Seniors, $3.00. Groups of 30 or more, $3.00 per person.

The Johnson House is a lesson in the American resistance to slavery; from its building in 1768 the house was home to three generations of a Quaker family who were important abolitionists. In the 1850s the house was a station on the Underground Railroad, offering all its building as shelter for African Americans escaping enslavement. Harriet Tubman herself was sheltered here, the most famous "conductor" on the railroad. Slave collars and ankle shackles are on display, vivid reminders of this injustice, as well as the secret compartments in the attic used to hide runaway slaves. One of the largest private homes in Philadelphia when it was built, the Johnson House attests to the economic and social standing of many Quakers. It stands three stories high, and its brick and stone exterior still bears damage from musket rounds and cannonballs fired during the Battle of Germantown in 1777. It was built by Jacob Knorr, a local joiner who also built Cliveden and the Concord School House (see both above).

LaSalle University Art Museum

1900 W. Olney Avenue (Map No. 3)
215-951-1221
www.lasalle.edu/services/art-mus

Open: Tu–F, 11:00 AM–4:00 PM; Su, 2:00 PM–4:00 PM. Call for special
summer hours
Admission: Free; Donation suggested

Designed to explore the history of the Western artistic tradition,
the collection is housed in the lower level of Olney Hall,
LaSalle's humanities and social sciences building on the main
campus. A series of six galleries organized by period invites visitors to consider the major styles and themes of Western art from
the Middle Ages to today through hundreds of paintings, prints,
drawings, and sculptures. Temporary exhibitions feature artifacts
from the museum's collection that are not on permanent display,
such as non-Western portraiture, Japanese prints, and Indian
miniatures.

Highlights:
Susan Dunleavy collection of illustrated and finely printed Bibles
Madonna and Child with the Cherries by Joos van Cleve
Virgil Reading the Aeneid before Augustus by Jean Auguste
Dominique Ingres

Laurel Hill

Edgeley Drive & Fairmount Avenue (Map No. 2)

215-235-1776

www.philamuseum.org/collections/parkhouse/laurelhill.shtml

Open: W–Su, 10:00 AM–4:00 PM (Jul. 1–Dec. 15); Sa–Su only (Apr. 1–Jun. 30)

Admission: $3.00

Built in the 1760s as a summer house, Laurel Hill is located on a high bluff overlooking the Schuylkill. Originally constructed as a symmetrical two-story Middle Georgian brick house with a main entry and a gallery of windows on the second floor, the house was subsequently enlarged with a single-story wing on the south side and a two-story octagonal wing on the north. The brick was covered with paint sometime in the late nineteenth century. The original builders of the house were loyalists, and Laurel Hill was briefly confiscated during the Revolutionary War. It was returned to their possession after the Treaty of Paris. The first floor is open to the public and contains period furnishings.

Highlights:

Delft tiles around the downstairs fireplace

A large porch offering an excellent view of Philadelphia

Lemon Hill

Kelly Drive & Sedgley Avenue, Fairmount Park East (Map No. 2)

215-232-4337

www.philamuseum.org/collections/parkhouse/lemonhill.shtml

Open: W–Su, 10:00 AM–4:00 PM (Apr. 1–Dec. 15)

Admission: $3.00

Lemon Hill takes its name from the greenhouses erected on the site by revolutionary financier and signer of the Declaration of Independence, Robert Morris, who maintained a working farm on the property. Morris was ruined by financial speculation, and the land was purchased at a sheriff's sale in 1799 by Henry Pratt, who built the elegant Federal-style stucco house that we know today. Like all the great museum houses preserved in Philadelphia, it is a stroke of luck that Lemon Hill has survived the centuries. The most interesting architectural aspect of this exquisite house is the stack of three oval rooms, a room style also found in the White House. In addition to the spectacular views the house affords, Lemon Hill also showcases excellent period furnishings.

Highlights:

The uncommon oval rooms interpreted with period furnishings

An entrance-hall checkerboard floor made of Valley Forge marble

A child's Windsor chair signed by Joseph Henzey, who made chairs for Independence Hall

The Library Company of Philadelphia

1314 Locust Street (Map No. 1)
215-546-3181
www.librarycompany.org
Open: M–F, 9:00 AM–4:45 PM
Admission: Free

Founded in the 1730s by Benjamin Franklin and other members
of the "Junto" as a way of sharing books, The Library Company
has grown into a world-renowned repository of documents and
related artifacts of pre–twentieth-century American history and
culture. With a collection of nearly 750,000 printed books,
graphics, and manuscripts, this Philadelphia institution is a major
resource for serious scholars. The Library Company has a small
permanent exhibition gallery of important artifacts of American
history and maintains temporary exhibits that feature some of the
important themes from its collection. The Library Company is
foremost a center of scholarly research, but visitors are encouraged to come by and enjoy the current exhibitions.

Living Loft Puppet Museum

3114 Spring Garden Street, 2nd Floor (Map No. 2)

215-222-6979

www.spiralq.org/livingLoft

Open: Please call to schedule a tour or workshop appointment

Admission: $5.00 per person (tour only); $12.00 per person (tour and one-hour workshop)

Part of the vibrant Spiral Q puppet workshop and theater, the Living Loft Puppet Museum is designed to allow visitors to understand the history and techniques behind one of the earliest forms of entertainment and social activism. The museum displays an incredible variety of puppets, masks, and props, ranging from gigantic puppets used for street demonstrations to delicate puppets of birds and fish. One of the highlights is a gigantic matador. In addition to a general tour, visitors have the option of a hands-on experience in the workshop where they can learn how puppets are made and used.

Marian Anderson Historical Residence and Museum

762 S. Marian Anderson Way (Map No. 1)

215-732-9505 or 856.966.1688

www.mariananderson.org

Open: Please call in advance for an appointment

Admission: Adults, $10.00; Children under 12 and Students, $5.00

Born in 1897 in Philadelphia, contralto Marian Anderson was the first African American to receive international acclaim as a classically trained singer. Her trailblazing performances occurred at Carnegie Hall, the White House, and major concert halls throughout the world. The great Italian conductor Arturo Toscanini told her that "Yours is a voice one hears once in a hundred years." In 1924 she purchased this modest brick row home in southwest Center City near her birthplace and the Union Baptist Church (1910 Fitzwater Street) where she learned to sing. The residence remained in her possession until her death in 1993 and contains memorabilia from her career.

Mario Lanza Museum

712 Montrose Street (Map No. 1)
215-238-9691
www.mario-lanza-institute.org

Open: M–Sa, 10:00 AM–3:00 PM
Admission: Free

Long before the "Three Tenors," this kid from the streets of
South Philly grew up to become America's first musical
crossover phenomenon, an opera singer who bridged the worlds
of classical and popular music. A tenor himself, Mario was born
Alfred Arnold Cocozza in 1921, the year that Caruso died, a
coincidence that Lanza later saw as a divine sign. While in his
twenties he signed a major deal with movie studio MGM and by
age 30 was one of the world's best-known singers. His early
death at age 39, in Rome, stunned his legions of fans. Today he is
remembered loyally by fans not only in Philadelphia, but all over
the world. Mario Lanza's music was featured most recently in
the movie *Heavenly Creatures*, directed by Peter Jackson of *Lord
of the Rings* fame. The museum in a South Philadelphia neighborhood contains many mementos and objects from his career,
including some of the stage costumes he wore.

Marvin Samson Center for the History of Pharmacy

University of the Sciences in Philadelphia (Map No. 2)
600 S. 43rd Street
215-596-8721
www.usip.edu

Open: M–F, 9:00 AM–5:00 PM
Admission: Free

As the Philadelphia College of Pharmacy was the first of its kind in North America, it is only fitting that the inheritor of this 1821 institution, the University of the Sciences in Philadelphia, should house the country's most extensive collection of artifacts and objects related to the creation and dispensation of drugs and medicines. Don't miss the murals on the walls outside the museum; they colorfully depict the history of pharmacy from Greco-Roman times to the present.

Highlights:
A historic collection of mortars and pestles
Botanical collections
Advertising material for patent medicines

The Masonic Library and Museum of Pennsylvania

1 N. Broad Street (Map No. 1)

215-988-1917

www.pagrandlodge.org

Open: Tu–F, 9:00 AM–5:00 PM; M, by appointment; Sa, 9:00 AM–noon (Closed Jul. & Aug.)

Admission: $3.00

With roots in the Middle Ages, the Brotherhood of Masons is a fraternity that has been part of American community life for over 250 years. Many of the Founding Fathers, including Benjamin Franklin, George Washington, John Hancock, and Paul Revere, were Masons. The influence of this organization is noteworthy in the early years of our country. Founded in 1908 and dedicated by John Wanamaker of department-store fame, the Lodge is housed in a National Historic Landmark building that contains seven halls, each built to exemplify a specific style of architecture. Try to make time for a guided tour of the halls (available at 11:00 AM, 2:00 PM, and 3:00 PM) to fully enjoy the architecture that includes ornate Italian Renaissance, Oriental, and Egyptian interpretations.

Highlights:

A Masonic apron presented to George Washington by Lafayette (Lafayette's wife did the embroidery)

Benjamin Franklin's Masonic sash

A thirteenth-century Templar's cross found in a Crusader's grave

Mennonite Meetinghouse

6133 Germantown Avenue (Map No. 3)
215-843-0943
www.meetinghouse.info

Open: Please call to arrange a tour
Admission: Adults, $3.00; Children, $2.00

The first permanent settlement of Mennonites was in
Philadelphia's Germantown. Erected in 1770, this fieldstone
meetinghouse, replacing an earlier one made from logs, is among
the oldest extant Mennonite buildings and is regarded as the
birthplace of Mennonites in America. William Rittenhouse (see
Historic Rittenhouse Town) was the first Mennonite minister in
the Colonies. Ardent abolitionists, the Mennonites allied themselves with the Quaker community to protest the institution of
slavery. Displays in the National Historic Landmark building
showcase Mennonite history and particularly its influence in the
antislavery movement in America.

Highlights:
A desk upon which was signed the first protest in the New
World against slavery in 1688
The old cemetery

Mother Bethel African Methodist Episcopal Church

419 S. Sixth Street (Map No. 1)

215-925-0616

www.holyexperiment.org/pages/bethel.html

Open: Tu–Sa, 10:00 AM–3:00 PM. Please call to arrange a tour.
Admission: Free

Built on the oldest parcel of land continuously owned by African Americans, Mother Bethel Church is the "mother church" of the nation's first black denomination. The congregation was formed in 1794 by Richard Allen, a slave who worked to pay for his freedom. Allen become a charismatic preacher who formed the Free African Society in 1787. Allen's ambition was to have a church for African Americans that was not an adjunct of a white church. Knowing that a place of worship was of premiere importance, he bought a wooden blacksmith shop and had it hauled by a team of horses to the corner of 6th and Lombard Streets, replacing it in 1805 with a stone structure. A brick church was erected on the site in 1841, ten years after Allen's death, while the present church, the fourth on the site, was begun in 1889 and dedicated in 1890. The church remains an active house of worship, so come prepared to respect the services.

Highlights:

An exhibit depicting the church's role as an Underground Railroad station

Richard Allen's bible, original pulpit, and tomb

Muskets from black troops mustered by Allen during the War of 1812

Mount Pleasant

Mount Pleasant Drive, Fairmount Park East (Map No. 2)
Phone: 215-684-7926
www.philamuseum.org/collections/parkhouse/mtpleasant.shtml

Open: Tu–Su, 10:00 AM–5:00 PM
Admission: $3.00

After having dined here in 1775 John Adams described Mount
Pleasant as "the most elegant seat in Pennsylvania." This historic
house still deserves lavish praise as one of the finest examples of a
Georgian country villa extant today. Undergoing a periodic
restoration, and soon to be reopened, everything from the woodwork to the furnishings reflect the work of master craftspeople,
and the fact that the original appearance of the house has been
maintained makes it of great architectural importance. Built by
Scottish sea captain John Macpherson in the 1760s, the house
also was briefly owned by Benedict Arnold. It was later purchased by General Jonathan Williams, a great-nephew of
Benjamin Franklin and the first superintendent of West Point
Military Academy, whose family retained the property until it
was acquired by the city. The furnishings are museum quality and
are placed to illuminate the elegant lifestyle of a moneyed family
in Colonial Philadelphia. For a taste of the history of the "lower
sort," visit the south pavilion, which has been made into a period
kitchen, complete with contemporary tools and kitchenware.

Highlights:
A Henry Maag tall case clock
A Thomas Affleck mahogany sideboard in the dining room
The Robert Waln library, exceptional for its integrity

Mummers Museum

1100 S. 2nd Street (Map No. 1)

215-336-3050

www.riverfrontmummers.com/museum.html

Open: Tu–Sa, 9:30 AM–4:30 PM; Su, noon–4:30 PM; Tu, to 9:30 PM
(May–Sep.); Closed Su (Jul.–Aug.)

Admission: Adults, $3.50; Children under 12, Students, and Seniors,
$2.50

New Year's Day celebrations are the closest Philadelphia comes
to Mardi Gras, thanks to the strutting, music-playing, sequined,
and costumed mummers whose annual parade attracts visitors
from around the world. This unique event has been officially
sanctioned by the city since 1901, although it is clear that mum-
mer-type celebrations have been part of the city's heritage since
colonial times. In addition to the string music, clowns, and fancy
costumes, this colorful, quintessential Philadelphia tradition
reflects the successful blend of practices from a variety of cultures, truly in the spirit of Brotherly Love. The showcase for the
history of the Mummers is their South Philadelphia museum,
which houses memorabilia, historic recordings, and designs for all
the themed marches.

Highlights:

A costume exhibit showing incredible handmade details

The Broad Street Room where visitors can learn the distinctive
Mummer's strut

Videos of notable performances of the past

Mütter Museum

College of Physicians of Philadelphia (Map No. 2)
19 S. 22nd Street
215-563-3737 ext. 211
www.collphyphil.org/muttpg1.shtml

Open: Daily, 10:00 AM–5:00 PM
Admission: Adults, $10.00; Children under 18, Seniors, and Students, $7.00

One of the most popular of the off-beat museums in the area, the Mütter Museum stands as a testament to the powerful draw of morbid curiosity. Established by Thomas Dent Mütter in 1856, the Museum was established to display medical oddities, and now boasts a truly astonishing collection of over 20,000 unique, curious, and—frankly—gruesome specimens. Squeamish visitors beware! Although these objects were collected in the interests of pure science, they bear witness to some very unusual variations of the human form: imagine coming face to face with a massive human colon, a wall of skulls, and preserved "monster" babies. Particularly noteworthy is the Museum's unrivaled collection of conjoined twins, both as specimens and in popular ephemera. There is more medical history available in the revolving exhibits at the College Gallery. If any family has teenagers who are bored with museums, a trip to the Mütter is a sure-fire cure!

Highlights:
The skeleton of a 7-foot-6-inch giant from Kentucky
A chair and other effects of conjoined twins Chang and Eng Bunker

National Constitution Center

525 Arch Street (Map No. 1)
215-409-6600
www.constitutioncenter.org

Open: M–F, 9:30 AM–5:00 PM; Sa & Su, to 6:00 PM
Admission: Adults, $6.00; Children 4–12 and Seniors, $5.00

Where else would the National Constitution Center be but in Philadelphia, the city where the document was drafted and signed? This addition to Independence National Historical Park was designed by the same architects who expanded the Louvre. The museum encourages visitors to see the Constitution as not just a historical document but as a flexible framework for a democratic, changing nation. It uses multimedia displays and interactive exhibits to allow visitors to explore the original conditions under which the Constitution was created and how changes and additions over time have further secured freedoms.

Highlights:

Signers Hall with 42 life-size bronze statues of the delegates to the Constitutional Convention in 1787

Freedom Rising, a 17-minute multimedia and live-action show that explains the basic points of the Constitution

National Liberty Museum

321 Chestnut Street (Map No. 1)
215-925-2800
www.libertymuseum.org

Open: Daily, 10:00 AM–5:00 PM (May 30–Sep. 1); Closed Mondays the remainder of the year.
Admission: Adults, $5.00; Seniors, $4.00; Students, $3.00

Right off Independence Mall is yet another institution dedicated to concepts that democracy holds dear. The eight galleries that comprise the National Liberty Museum explore the nature of freedom and the responsibilities and sacrifices of citizens in a free society. The artwork on display includes conceptual glass pieces by Dale Chihuly, Czeslaw Zuber, and Peter Yenawine that symbolize the fragile quality of freedom. One of the museum's strengths are the exhibits that allow visitors to understand how obstacles to liberty like bigotry and violence have been overcome by successive groups of Americans.

Highlights:
An exhibit about the experiences of immigrants to America
A hands-on exhibit to explore peaceful conflict resolution
A presidential china collection

National Museum of American Jewish History

55 N. 5th Street (Map No. 1)

215-923-3811

www.nmajh.org

Open: M–Th, 10:00 AM–5:00 PM; F, 10:00 AM–3:00 PM; Su, noon–5:00 PM

Admission: Adults, $4.00; Seniors and Children, $3.00 (main gallery)

The only museum in the country dedicated to preserving and interpreting artifacts on the 300-year Jewish experience in America, the National Museum of American Jewish History currently shares space with the historic Congregation Mikveh Israel, the "Synagogue of the American Revolution." The collection of more than 10,000 artifacts, including documents, photographs, ritual items, artwork, and personal items allows visitors to understand the long-standing and important history of Jewish people and culture in the United States.

New Hall Military Museum

320 Chestnut Street (Map No. 1)
215-965-2305
www.nps.gov/inde/new-hall.html
Open: Daily, 2:00 PM–5:00 PM
Admission: Free

The New Hall Military Museum is housed in a recreation of the building built by the Carpenters' Company in 1791 for the office of the First Secretary of War and his staff. The museum is dedicated to early American military history, and here the visitor can learn, for instance, that the United States Marines were actually created a half year before the Declaration of Independence was written. The first floor concentrates on the history of the Marines, with time lines explaining their role at pivotal moments in the American Revolution, such as Washington's crossing of the Delaware and the surprise attack on Hessian troops at Trenton. The second floor is dedicated to the Army and Navy in the war of independence and their surprising fate immediately after the revolution. Fearing a standing military, soldiers and sailors were disbanded, and the Army dwindled to just 87 soldiers! But the quasi-war with France and the War of 1812 gave these institutions the permanent standing they have today.

Highlights:
One of the oldest American flags in existence, circa 1780
A diorama depicting the establishment of the Continental Marine Corps at Philadelphia's Tun Tavern in 1775
Eighteenth-century uniforms and weapons

Paul Robeson House

4949 Walnut Street (Map No. 2)
215-747-4675
www.wpcalliance.org

Open: Please call in advance for an appointment
Admission: Free

The son of a former slave, Paul Robeson became only the third black student to win an academic scholarship to Rutgers University. In 1919 he graduated as his class valedictorian. He then went on to earn a law degree from Columbia in 1923. Prejudice and discrimination in this career led him to explore entertainment, and he became world renowned for his parts in films like *Showboat* that included his classic rendition of "Old Man River." He toured the world giving concerts, but like fellow vocalist with Philadelphia connections, Marian Anderson, he faced acceptance abroad but discrimination at home. His speaking publicly about bigotry in the United States and support for socialist causes led the House Committee on Un-American Activities to denounce him as a communist in 1947, and the State Department denied him a passport until 1958, essentially ruining his career. In the 1960s, Robeson moved to Philadelphia and lived in seclusion at this house until his death in 1976. Maintained by the West Philadelphia Cultural Alliance, the house traces Robeson's sobering life story in family pictures, memorabilia, and an audiovisual display to honor his legacy as a testament to courage and resolution.

Pennsylvania Academy of the Fine Arts

118 N. Broad Street (Map No. 1)

215-972-7600

www.pafa.org

Open: Tu–Sa, 10:00 AM–5:00 PM; Su, 11:00 AM–5:00 PM

Admission: Adults, $5.95; Seniors and Students, $4.95; Children under 12, $3.95; Children under 5, Free. Groups: Adults, $6.95; Other rates same. Call for lunch tour rates.

A visit to the Pennsylvania Academy of Fine Arts, one of the most influential institutions in the history of American art, should be on any art-lover's itinerary. The nation's first art museum and art academy, it was founded in 1805 by painter and scientist Charles Wilson Peale, sculptor William Rush, and other influential Philadelphia personalities. In a letter to President Thomas Jefferson, Peale wrote of his hopes to establish "an Academy for the encouragement of the fine arts." The current building was designed by Frank Furness and built in 1876. The collection contains some of the most recognizable paintings in American art and ranges from early national artists like the Peales, Benjamin West, William Merritt Chase, and Childe Hassam to nineteenth-century icons like Winslow Homer, Mary Cassatt, and Thomas Eakins. Contemporary artists are also a strength of the collection, as visitors can see works by the likes of Frank Stella and Richard Diebenkorn.

Highlights:

Charles Wilson Peale's *The Artist in His Museum*

Benjamin West's *Penn's Treaty with the Indians*

Edward Hicks' *Peaceable Kingdom*

Pennsylvania Hospital

800 Spruce Street (Map No. 1)

215-829-3270

www.uphs.upenn.edu/paharc/tour/index.html

Open: M–F, 8:30 AM–4:30 PM; for a guided tour, please call ahead.

Admission: Free

Although it is a large urban hospital, Pennsylvania Hospital takes its legacy as the first hospital in America very seriously (Benjamin Franklin was one of the founders) and welcomes visitors to explore its architecture, artifacts, and grounds. Its impressive collection is housed in the Pine Building, an eighteenth-century brick Federal building. A self-guided tour is available from the Welcome Desk off the 8th Street entrance. Guided tours are also available if you call ahead, and your visit will be enhanced with the aid of a guide. Do not miss the fascinating Surgical Amphitheater, built in 1804, the oldest existing one in the country. This circular room could hold up to 130 students and observers to watch surgical procedures performed without benefit of anesthesia (until 1840). Benjamin West's magnificent *Christ Healing the Sick in the Temple* is said to be the first piece of fine art publicly displayed in colonial America. During its first year of showing in 1817, it attracted 30,000 visitors. Thomas Scully's portrait of Benjamin Rush, signer of the Declaration of Independence and the father of American psychiatry, is also on display. The hospital gardens are worth a visit as well, as they contain a recreated eighteenth-century herbal garden with clearly marked plants.

Pennsylvania Convention Center

1101 Arch Street (Map No. 1)

215-418-4735

www.paconvention.com

Open: Daily; Please call for a guided tour

Admission: Free

Both *The New York Times* and *Art in America* have written glow-ingly of the contemporary art collection at the Convention Center. Consistently remarked upon by convention visitors, this collection is not as well known by the general public as it should be. Comprising more than 100 works, mostly by artists with con-nections to Pennsylvania, the collection is displayed throughout the Convention Center and represents a range of media from sculptures, paintings, and installations to woodwork and jewelry. Particularly noteworthy is the hanging sculpture in the Great Hall, including a massive 40-foot-long sculpture of spoons, cups, and bowls. While you're visiting, take time to admire two archi-tectural wonders, the arched roof over the Great Hall and Ballroom—the only one of its kind in the nation—and the only remaining single-span arched train shed in America, incorporated from the old Reading Terminal, whose market full of delicious foods from around the world is next door. Guided tours are available by appointment.

Philadelphia Beauty Showcase National Historical Museum

510-514 S. 52nd Street (Map No. 2)

215-474-7533

www.pbsnhm.com

Open: M–Sa, 10:00 AM–4:30 PM; Please call in advance for a tour

Admission: $6.75; Call for group rates

Founded in 2002, this museum is dedicated to the history of both the beauty industry and the different cultural forms beauty has taken across time. Philadelphia has been a center for beauty-product development and techniques, and the museum reflects many of these local innovations and success stories. Visitors can enjoy a large number of historical artifacts dealing with hair styling, makeup, and grooming. Exhibits highlight key historical styles and trends, and these are enhanced by audio-visual presentations.

Philadelphia Contributionship for the Insurance of Houses from Loss by Fire

212 S. 4th Street (Map No. 1)

215-627-1752

www.contributionship.com/about.html

Open: M–F, 9:00 AM–4:00 PM. Tours of the upper rooms are available if arrangements are made in advance.

Admission: Free

The oldest fire insurance company in America, founded by Benjamin Franklin and other like-minded citizens, is still in business after 250 years. You can find the firm's famous fire mark—four hands intertwined—on some of the older homes of the city. The original bronze fire mark was cast by John Stow, who recast the Liberty Bell. Partly because Philadelphia actively prepared for fire prevention and partly because of luck, Philadelphia has never suffered a major fire in its history, and as a result, many buildings that might have otherwise perished have survived for centuries. The company maintains a museum of fire memorabilia on the first floor of its offices in this 1836 brick building in Old City. If you plan ahead, you can see the second-floor rooms, resplendent with exquisite furnishings of bird's-eye maple, marble fireplaces, and crystal chandeliers.

Highlights:

A rare silver "speaking trumpet" used to broadcast orders at fire sites

Surveys for the homes of William Penn's son and Benjamin Franklin

A collection of miniature fire engines

Philadelphia Doll Museum

2253 N. Broad Street (Map No. 2)
215-787-0220
www.philadollmuseum.com

Open: Th–Sa, 10:00 AM–4:00 PM; Su, noon–4:00 PM
Admission: Adults, $4.00; Seniors, Students, and Children under 12, $3.00. Group rates and tours are available

The Philadelphia Doll Museum is a doll-lover's dream. The museum is the only one in the world that collects and interprets black dolls for their role in world history and culture. The astonishing collection of 500 black dolls include West African carved dolls, nineteenth-century European bisque dolls, and American dolls of the late twentieth century created in response to the civil rights movement.

Highlights:

German-made papier-mâché black dolls from the early nineteenth century

A complete set of Robert Bell African American heritage dolls

Philadelphia Insectarium

8046 Frankford Avenue (Map No. 3)
215-338-3000
www.insectarium.com

Open: M–Sa, 10:00 AM–4:00 PM
Admission: $5.00; Children under 3, Free

What started as a marketing tool to bring in foot traffic is now a hugely popular museum that provides enough "ick" factor to bring the kids in by droves. Steve's Bug Off Exterminating Company in the Northeast used to showcase a "catch of the day" in their front window, a traffic-stopper that grew into the three-floor Insectarium, the largest insect museum in the country, where visitors can view live and mounted insects from all over the world. The emphasis is on the important roles played by these tiny citizens of the natural world, and their pervasiveness on the earth—insects are the most numerous of any living group of animals. The Insectarium gives a good introduction to the diversity of the insect world, with a huge collection of butterflies to specialty collections of poisonous bugs and other insectlike creatures, such as spiders, tarantulas, and scorpions. Interactive displays allow you to learn about the how fast insects are, how long they can live, and how many are born from a single female.

Highlights:
Tanks containing live rare and unusual insects and spiders
A working beehive
A step-by-step display of how a spider engineers its web

Philadelphia Jewish Sports Hall of Fame

The Gershman Y, 401 S. Broad Street (Map No. 1)
215-446-3036
www.pjshf.com
Open: Su–F, 10:00 AM–4:00 PM
Admission: Free

This two-room museum is chock-full of Jewish contributions to sports, both on and off the playing field. With a heavy emphasis on basketball, the collection shows how this game in particular held an attraction for young urban Jewish men of the 1930s, as it offered an opportunity to break out of their poor neighborhoods and engage in a broadening activity that could lead to a college scholarship. The displays highlight individual contributions, like Harry Litwack, the Temple basketball coach responsible for inventing the zone defense; Randy Grossman, tight end on four Pittsburgh Steeler Super Bowl championship teams; and "Battling Levinsky," who held the light heavyweight championship from 1916 to 1920. One room features plaques that offer brief biographies of the persons who have been inducted — players, coaches, agents, owners, and broadcasters — including numerous Olympic stars and All-Americans.

Highlights:
A display dedicated to the 1972 Munich Olympic tragedy

Philadelphia Museum of Art

26th Street & the Benjamin Franklin Parkway (Map No. 2)

215-763-8100

www.philamuseum.org

Open: Tu–Su, 10:00 AM–5:00 PM; F, –8:45 PM

Admission: Adults, $10.00; Seniors, Students, and Children 13–18, $7.00; Children under 12, Free

In a city with so many great museums, it is fitting that Philadelphia's primary art museum is both the most conspicuous—easily recognized on its bluff along the Schuylkill as it presides over the Benjamin Franklin Parkway—and the city's most renowned institution, a museum that is among the finest in the world. Constructed in 1928 after a Greek temple design, the Philadelphia Museum of Art covers nearly ten acres with its 200 galleries. Lovers of trivia will note that the building was designed by Julian Francis Abele, the first African American to graduate from the University of Pennsylvania School of Architecture. This is a museum not to be missed. The galleries are grouped by period, giving the visitor the chance to appreciate both the fine and decorative arts from the third millennium BC to the present. The museum has strengths in many areas, including Renaissance, Impressionist, Asian, American, and modern artworks, furniture, arms and armor, costumes, and oriental carpets. It is also home to the leading Dadaist collection in the world, including an entire wing devoted to Marcel Duchamp's works. Its famous reconstructed cultural and historical rooms are treats, allowing visitors to stroll through centuries and travel around the world all within the museum's walls. Don't miss the Buddhist temple, the Japanese teahouse, or the thirteenth-century French cloister.

Paintings and sculpture are at the core of the museum's collection, and there are hundreds of priceless treasures including *The Three Musicians* and the 1906 *Self Portrait* by Picasso, *Dog Barking at the Moon* by Miró, *Soft Construction with Boiled Beans* by Dalí, *The Large Bathers* by Cézanne, *The Birth of Venus* by Poussin, and *A Huntsman and Dogs* by Homer. The museum is also host to special exhibits, many of which receive national and international attention. It is worth checking ahead to see what the current exhibit is in order to secure tickets.

Additional Highlights:
An arms & armor collection
The colonial furniture collection
Marcel Duchamp's *Nude Descending a Staircase*

Philadelphia Museum of Judaica at Rodeph Shalom

615 N. Broad Street (Map No. 2)

215-627-6747

www.rodephshalom.org/museum

Open: M–Th, 10:00 AM–4:00 PM; F, 10:00 AM–2:00 PM; Su, 10:00 AM–noon

Admission: Free

Housed in an elegant Frank Furness building, Rodeph Shalom was founded in 1795 and is the oldest Ashkenazic congregation in the United States. The Rodeph Shalom museum features more than 500 international objects and artifacts, the core of which is The Leon J. and Julia S. Obermayer Collection of Ritual Jewish Art. The permanent collection is often augmented by traveling exhibits of contemporary works. The stained-glass windows in the sanctuary are by renowned artist Nicola D'Ascenzo.

Philadelphia Sketch Club

235 S. Camac Street (Map No. 1)
215-545-9298
www.sketchclub.org
Open: M, W, F, Sa, Su, 1:00 PM–5:00 PM (Closed Jul. & Aug.)
Admission: Free

Founded in 1860 by Bohemian students of the Pennsylvania Academy of Fine Arts, the Sketch Club is the oldest artists' organization in the United States. Its members, which have included Thomas Eakins and Maxfield Parrish, wanted a place where they could freely explore their creative intuition, and at that time this meant sketching, or illustrating, rather than painting or sculpting. Housed in three Federal period row houses that have been connected, the collection features works in all mediums by the renowned members over the years, and they are displayed along with an eclectic mix of wooden ship models, stained-glass windows, pottery, and antique iron work that have been presented to the club over its history. Still dedicated to showcasing contemporary art, important regional artists often have exhibits here of their latest works.

Philadelphia University–The Design Center

4200 Henry Avenue (Map No. 2)

215-951-2860

www.philau.edu/designcenter

Open: M–F, 10:00 AM–4:00 PM; Please call for an appointment

Admission: Free

The Design Center at Philadelphia University is home to one of the largest textile collections in the United States. The collection documents Western and non-Western textiles and costumes from the first century AD to the present, representing nearly every country in the world. A special feature of the collection is an extraordinary assembly of nineteenth- and early twentieth-century textiles, textile-related artifacts, and tools that document the emergence of Philadelphia as one of the country's major textile producers of the time. Fashion designers and those interested in specific textile arts, such as lacework, regularly consult the collection. The Design Center's building, the former residence of Goldie Paley, mother of William Paley, the founder of CBS, is itself remarkable as an example of mid-twentieth-century architecture.

Physick House

321 S. 4th Street (Map No. 1)

215-925-7866

www.philalandmarks.org/page_houses/physick/home/

Hours: Th–Sa, noon–5:00 PM; Su, 1:00 PM–5:00 PM; Hourly tours

Admission: Adults and Children 8 and over, $5.00; Seniors and Students, $3.00

This four-story brick house was built in 1786 by wealthy wine importer Henry Hill, the executor of Benjamin Franklin's will, but it is known by the name of its most famous resident, Dr. Philip Syng Physick, the "Father of American Surgery." One of the few influential people to stay in the city during the yellow fever outbreaks of the 1790s, Physick earned the respect of the town by this noble action and by his contributions to the comfort of his fellow citizens. He pioneered the use of the stomach pump, was one of the first to use autopsy as a further means of investigation, performed some of the earliest cataract surgeries, and created the first carbonated soft drink in this country as a means of relieving gastric distress, using the method developed by Schweppes in England. The second floor of his house is set aside as a medical museum. The first floor is decorated in the Federal period with the exquisite trappings one would find in a house of the well-to-do of the early nineteenth century.

Highlights:

A fanlight (the largest of its time) over the front door

Furnishings in the style of Rome (the ruins of Pompeii had just been discovered)

A garden planted in the manner of the time

Please Touch Museum

210 N. 21st Street (Map No. 1)
215-963-0667
www.pleasetouchmuseum.org

Open: Daily, 9:00 AM–4:30 PM; to 5:00 PM (Jul.–Sep.)
Admission: Adults and Children, $9.95; Children under one year, Free

Started by Montessori educators, the Please Touch Museum is designed specifically for children under the age of 7. The museum encourages a child's own instinct for curiosity and exploration by featuring lots of interactive displays. There is an incredible variety of things for children to do, such as the Move It exhibit where children can navigate waterways with toy boats, pretend to drive vehicles, and climb aboard a monorail; a grocery store where children can pretend to shop; and the Mad Hatter's tea party with plenty of empty seats for children who want to join in the fun. Other exhibits include Kids Construct, which teaches children about architecture and building, and a special farm designed to stimulate motor skills in children under 3. The museum has also set aside a special place for quiet reading. The power of play leads children to learn concepts of science, modes of transportation, broadcasting, and a host of other contemporary wonders in this imaginatively conceived space for families.

Polish American Cultural Center Museum

308 Walnut Street (Map No. 1)
215-922-1700
www.polishamericancenter.org
Open: M–F, 10:00 AM–4:00 PM (Jan.–Apr.); M–Sa, 10:00 AM–4:00 PM (May–Dec.)
Admission: Free

The Cultural Center honors Polish customs, folk art, traditions, and famous figures of Polish descent. Displays highlight internationally known personalities like Frederic Chopin, Madame Curie, Nicholas Copernicus, and Lech Walesa as well as ones of particular interest to America like Thaddeus Kosciuszko and Casimir Pulaski. Both Kosciuszko and Pulaski were influential during the revolutionary period. Count Pulaski trained the Continental Army in cavalry techniques and even funded the effort when the young nation's resources were low, while Kosciuszko brought his brilliant military engineering expertise to the aid of the Americans and is credited for establishing key battlefield advantages at Saratoga and West Point.

Highlights:
An exhibit on the Polish military experience of World War II
Pisanki, traditional painted Easter eggs

Powel House

244 S. 3rd Street (Map No. 1)

215-627-0364

www.philalandmarks.org/page_houses/powel/home/index.html

Open: Th–Sa, noon–5:00 PM; Su, 1:00 PM–5:00 PM

Admission: Adults, $5.00; Seniors and Students, $4.00; Groups of ten or more, $3.00 per person; Families, $12.00; Children 6 and under, Free

This elegant 1765 brick house welcomed luminaries of the Age of Revolution, yet without civic preservation efforts, we may have been left with a parking lot rather than one of the finest Georgian townhouses in America. Much of the interior was sold off before the house was saved from demolition, but over the past 70 years the house has been painstakingly refurbished and recreated to represent what it may have been like during the late eighteenth century. Purchased in 1769 by Samuel Powel, the last mayor of Philadelphia under the crown and the first under the new republic, the house was the scene of frequent gatherings of key figures, including Benjamin Franklin, George Washington, John Adams, and the Marquis de Lafayette. Powel and his wife became such friends to the first presidential couple, in fact, that the Washingtons celebrated their twentieth wedding anniversary here. The house was apparently the first in the city to have a dining parlor, and one might imagine the sparkling conversations over many-course meals. The upstairs ballroom where George and Martha danced and Lafayette was feted showcases several rare musical instruments.

Highlights:

A set of Nanking china from George and Martha Washington

Presbyterian Historical Society

425 Lombard Street (Map No. 1)
215-627-1852
www.history.pcusa.org/about/phila.html

Open: M–F, 8:30 AM–4:30 PM
Admission: Free

Founded in 1852, the Presbyterian Historical Society has an extensive library of books and manuscripts related to the history of the Presbyterian sect in America and a small museum dedicated to important Presbyterian contributions to American history.

Highlights:

A tall case clock belonging to John Witherspoon, the only minister to sign the Declaration of Independence

Rembrandt Peale portraits

Alexander Calder statues flanking the garden

Rodin Museum

Benjamin Franklin Parkway at 22nd Street (Map No. 2)
215-763-8100
www.rodinmuseum.org

Open: Tu–Su, 10:00 AM–5:00 PM
Admission: $3.00

This collection of works by the great French sculptor, the most complete outside of Paris, is here in Philadelphia thanks to Jules E. Mastbaum, a movie theater magnate and well-known philanthropist. Opened to the public in 1924 along the Benjamin Franklin Parkway — an avenue inspired by the Avenue des Champs-Elysées in Paris, the temple-like building houses 124 sculptures, including bronze casts of the artist's greatest works, as well as drawings, paintings, and studies by the most famous sculptor of the nineteenth century. The gardens surrounding the museum provide a romantic atmosphere to contemplate Rodin's masterpieces. The bronze cast of the artist's last, and unfinished, work, *The Gates of Hell*, form the doorway arch of the main entranceway.

Highlights:
A bronze cast of *The Thinker*
Photos of the artist by Edward Steichen
A bronze cast of *The Kiss*

Romanian Folk Art Museum

1606 Spruce Street (Map No. 1)
215-732-6780
http://users.erols.com/romuseum/

Open: Please call in advance for an appointment
Admission: $4.00

The Romanian Museum, founded in Chicago and based in Philadelphia for 19 years, is the largest collection of Romanian folk artifacts outside of Romania. The museum features folk furniture, religious objects, and decorated eggs; but the core of the collection is in textiles, including colorful wool blankets, bedcovers, wall hangings, tablecloths, pillowcases, and decorative runners. Finely carved and painted cupboards and dowry chests show the rich folk heritage of the region. The permanent collection also contains hundreds of pieces made by contemporary Romanian artisans. There is also a branch museum with more costumes and textiles in Princeton.

Highlights:
Rare nineteenth-century icons painted on glass
A large collection of painted and beaded Easter eggs
Glazed terra cotta tiles made by eighteenth-century monks in a Transylvania monastery

Rosenbach Museum and Library

2008-2010 Delancy Place (Map No. 2)
215-732-1600
www.rosenbach.org

Open Tu–Su, 10:00 AM–5:00 PM; W, –8:00 PM
Admission: Adults, $8.00; Seniors and Students, $5.00; Children under
5, $3.00

A showcase to an inspired collection amassed by two brothers
who were fine-arts and rare-book dealers, the Rosenbach
Museum is housed in their 1860s townhouse and an adjoining
building now connected to the museum to make room for the
collection. Visitors of all tastes will want to spend an afternoon
here, as the museum is home to one of the nation's finest collections of rare books and manuscripts and a noteworthy collection
of furniture, silver, paintings, prints, drawings, and sculpture.
Important pieces of colonial furniture and portraiture share space
with Roman sculpture, William Blake prints, and a first edition
of *Poor Richard's Almanack*. The Rosenbach Museum and
Library remains active in community outreach and education.

Highlights:
James Joyce's handwritten *Ulysses*
The largest collection of drawings by children's author Maurice
Sendak
Notes and outlines for *Dracula*, Bram Stoker's masterpiece
Thomas Jefferson's draft of the Declaration of Independence

The Robert W. Ryerss Library and Museum

Burholme Park, 7370 Central Avenue (Map No. 3)

215-685-0544 / 215-685-0599

www.philaparks.org/ppaary.htm

Open: F–Su, 10:00 AM–4:00 PM

Admission: Free

Built in the mid-nineteenth century, Burholme, an Italianate mansion, is surrounded by 70 acres of beautiful parkland. Once the private home of railroad magnate Joseph Waln Ryerss and his family, the property was opened as a public museum and library in 1910. The Waln-Ryerss family were world travelers throughout the nineteenth century, and they amassed an important collection of artifacts, mainly from Native American and Asian cultures. In the 1920s, a two-story addition was built off the main house to serve as a more formal museum to showcase these treasures. The house is currently arranged to convey how rooms might have looked when occupied by the Ryerss family—full of interesting furniture, art, and curios—although some room partitions have been replaced with columns to better support the library on the second floor. The library is open to the public and serves the surrounding community. Anyone with an interest in Victorian style or Asian art should make time to visit Burholme.

Highlights:

Japanese temple furniture

A large Buddha sculpture

Unusual weapons, musical instruments, and cooking utensils

Native American artifacts

Second Bank of the United States

420 Chestnut Street (Map No. 1)
215-965-2305
www.nps.gov/inde/second-bank.html

Open: Daily, 9:00 AM–4:00 PM
Admission: Free

Inspired by the Parthenon and designed by William Strickland, the Second Bank of the United States has lent its neoclassical design to countless bank buildings across the country. The bank was founded in 1816 during James Madison's administration in response to rising inflation caused by private banks seeking to capitalize on the huge government debt incurred from the War of 1812. Provided with a charter lasting 20 years, the bank, under the direction of Philadelphian Nicholas Biddle, became the most powerful financial institution in the country and appeared to threaten the authority of state banks and even the government. Ultimately Andrew Jackson, in a bitter dispute with Biddle, vetoed the recharter of the Second Bank, and the commercial center of the United States moved from Philadelphia to Wall Street. Closed for a period while being renovated, the bank has reopened and visitors can once again enjoy the important collection of portraits of the colonial era, an invaluable guide for placing famous names with faces.

Highlights:
Washington's death mask
A Patrick Henry portrait
A General Lafayette portrait

SEPTA Museum

1234 Market Street (Map No. 1)
215-580-7168
www.septa.org/store.html

Open: M–F, 9:30 AM–5:00 PM; Sa, 10:00 AM–3:00 PM
Admission: Free

For the daily commuter, the Southeastern Pennsylvania Transit Authority simply provides the means to get to and from the city. For the rail buff, though, it is an endless source of fascination. Dedicated to the history of the Philadelphia area's transit system, the SEPTA museum tells the story of public transportation as it grew along with one of the largest metropolitan regions in the country. Featuring transit ephemera and restored vintage train and trolley cars, this little museum is a sure bet for anyone interested in transportation and technology in general. The museum store features a great collection of videos, books, magazines, and models.

Highlights:
A 1947 trolley car
Historic time cards, tickets, and posters

Shoe Museum

Temple University School of Podiatry (Map No. 2)
8th & Race Streets
215-625-5243
http://podiatry.temple.edu/shoe_museum/shoe_museum.html

Open: Please call in advance for an appointment
Admission: Free

Shoes protect feet from injury, wear, and fatigue, of course, but because we wear shoes they are one of our most conspicuous fashion accents. Philadelphia is home to one of the few museums in the country dedicated to footwear, and it is well worth making a call to set up an appointment. Of the nearly 1,000 pairs of shoes in this amazing collection, at least 250 pairs are always on display. Featuring footwear from more than 30 nations, the course of human history and civilizations can be traced, from Egyptian burial sandals, Malaysian clogs, and Eskimo boots to modern athletic designs. The museum is also home to a variety of celebrity and costume footwear, such as Ella Fitzgerald's gold boots, Reggie Jackson's five-home-run World Series shoes, and the '70s platforms worn by Sallie Struthers in the television show *All in the Family*. If you enjoy fashion, you shouldn't miss the opportunity to schedule a tour of this shrine to one of the most distinctive and interesting aspects of human clothing.

Highlights:
Chinese "lily" shoes created for the bound foot
Authentic wooden sabots, the shoes that gave us the word sabotage

Shofuso

North Horticultural Drive, Fairmount Park (Map No. 2)
215-878-5097
www.shofuso.com

Open: Tu–F, 10:00 AM–4:00 PM; Sa & Su, 11:00 AM–5:00 PM
Admission: Adults, $4.00; Seniors and Students, $3.00

Although Shofuso, "Pine Breeze House,"(or the Japanese House as it is commonly called) was built in the mid-1950s, the ground upon which it stands has held a Japanese-inspired exhibit since the 1876 Centennial celebration. The current house was built by the America-Japan Society and given to the Metropolitan Museum of Art, which donated the building to Philadelphia in 1958. Characterizing an upper-class house of the seventeenth century, the house is built of a lightweight hinoki wood without any structural nails, the main building resting on a platform. The style is called "shoin-zukuri," or desk centered, and is a wonder of harmony and peace, with the gardens leading seamlessly into the light-filled airy structure. Inside, sliding rice paper panels set off the large main room from the sleeping room, dirt-floored kitchen, and the tea house, which is entered from a wooden bridge.

Highlights:
A seventeenth-century "dago" or "kago" sedan chair
A replica of a Japanese wooden bath
An ornamental garden and pond

Stenton

4601 N. 18th Street (Map No. 2)
215-329-7312
www.stenton.org

Open: Tu–Sa, 1:00 PM–4:00 PM (Apr. 1–Dec. 15)
Admission: Adults, $3.00; Children, $1.50

Being "heartily out of love with this world," James Logan, secretary to William Penn, built the magnificent country estate, Stenton, in 1730 on 500 acres as his home of retirement. Such was his reputation in the colonies, however, that the world soon came to him, and his 20-year occupancy was distinguished by visits from the likes of Benjamin Franklin, John Bartram, and Native American chiefs. Now situated on three acres, the house is still a commanding presence with its symmetric brick exterior and elegant interiors, one of the earliest and best examples of the Georgian style in the New World. It was so well preserved by the generations of Logans that electricity and plumbing were never installed until the Colonial Dames took over stewardship in the twentieth century. The house is furnished with museum-quality pieces; the Logans commissioned many works from the most famous furniture makers of their day and imported pieces from England. The resulting collection is a marvelously coherent group of eighteenth-century material goods and decorative arts, ranging from textiles and clothing to furniture and painting.

Highlights:
A "whispering closet" where servants could listen to visitors before the Stentons joined their guests
A barn with early American farm tools

Stephen Girard Collection

Girard College (Map No. 2)
2101 S. College Avenue
215-787-2680
www.girardcollege.com/aboutus/history.html

Open: Th, 10:00 AM–2:00 PM; Tours by reservation at other times
Admission: Free

Just eight blocks away from the Philadelphia Museum of Art is one of America's best collections of fine and decorative arts from the early national period, housed in a stunning Greek Revival temple called Founder's Hall at the heart of the Girard College campus. Founder's Hall was built by the same architect who designed portions of the United States Capitol and was once the second most expensive building erected in America—the Capitol was the first. Stephen Girard was a French-born mariner, merchant, banker, and America's first multimillionaire. He was so wealthy, in fact, that during the War of 1812 he helped finance the insolvent American government. Upon his death he bequeathed his fortune to start the school that still bears his name, and also gave the school his possessions, including fine furniture, ceramics, silver, textiles, paintings, and prints, that are now on display at Founder's Hall. Despite the fact that the museum is only open on Thursdays for walk-in visits, a phone call can allow you to arrange a tour on other days, and it is well worth the effort to see this exquisite historical collection.

Highlights:

A nearly complete set of ebony parlor furniture made by Ephraim Haines

A musical Secrétaire à Abattant that plays wooden rolls

Strawberry Mansion

33rd & Dauphin Streets, Fairmount Park East (Map No. 2)
215-228-8364
www.philamuseum.org/collections/parkhouse/strawberry.shtml

Open: W–Su, 10:00 AM–4:00 PM
Admission: $3.00

Originally a Federal-style country house named Summerville built in 1790 on the site of an existing house, the house was significantly expanded in the 1820s with the addition of large Greek Revival wings. It wasn't until the mid-nineteenth century that the house became known as Strawberry Mansion, so called because it was associated with serving strawberries and cream to pleasure boaters along the Schuylkill. The house ultimately became property of the city, and like several other historic houses in Fairmount Park, it is embellished with period furnishing provided by the Philadelphia Museum of Art. From the visitors' initial impression of the unusual entrance hall with its four statuary niches and fanlights, the house continues to surprise with the formal reception room in neoclassical style that features a circular "chatting couch," the exquisite Tucker porcelain displayed in the library, and the attic full of antique toys.

Highlights:
An antique toy collection, including eighteenth-century baby carriages and ice skates
A collection of Tucker porcelain, one of the first true porcelains made in America

Sweetbrier

Fairmount Park West (Map No. 2)

215-222-1333

www.philamuseum.org/collections/parkhouse/sweetbriar.shtml

Open: W–Su, 10:00 AM–4:00 PM (Jul. 1–Dec. 15)

Admission: $3.00

The latter part of the eighteenth century saw a move toward more refined, classically inspired designs, and Sweetbrier (sometimes spelled Sweetbriar), completed in 1797, is a beautifully rendered example of this. Its stone exterior, although somewhat altered over the years, is ornamented with quoins; long floor-to-ceiling windows on the first-floor drawing room and the wide main passage lend an open, airy feeling to the interior. Samuel Breck, the original owner, was an influential Philadelphia merchant, educated in France, who eventually served in Pennsylvania state government. The current interior interpretation is designed to reflect what would have been Breck's refined tastes. Of particular interest is a double parlor on the first floor furnished in the Etruscan style, which was popular in Europe at the time. Breck sold the house in 1838, and 30 years later, the house and grounds were acquired by the city.

Highlights:

Important Philadelphia-made furniture

A chandelier bought from the Aga Khan's palace

Taller Puertorriqueño

2721 N. 5th Street (Map No. 2)
215-426-3311
www.tallerpr.org

Open: Tu–Sa, 10:00 AM–6:00 PM
Admission: Free

Begun as a community center and space to develop and promote
Puerto Rican artistic and cultural traditions throughout
Philadelphia, Taller Puertorriqueño (Puerto Rican workshop) has
since broadened its mission to include works by other Latin
American and Caribbean artists. This dynamic organization hosts
exhibits by contemporary artists and maintains a permanent collection of painting, sculpture, works on paper, and video arts.

Thaddeus Kosciuszko National Memorial

3rd & Pine Streets (Map No. 1)
215-597-9618
www.nps.gov/thko
Open: W–Su, 10:00 AM–5:00 PM
Admission: Free

Most Americans have never heard of Thaddeus Kosciuszko, but he was one of the first European volunteers to aid the American cause. A military engineer and officer from Poland, Kosciuszko selected the site and designed the first fortifications of what would become West Point. These fortifications are credited with preventing a British advance out of New York City that might have changed the course of the war. Kosciuszko returned to his native Poland to fight for its independence, but despite a victory over the Russians in 1794, Kosciusko was eventually forced to surrender. Severely wounded and placed in a Russian prison, he was pardoned and returned to the United States in 1797. Kosciuszko rented a room in this house in Old City, and it now serves as a memorial to his services to America. Here, for several months, he entertained visitors of all backgrounds and social stations, most notably Thomas Jefferson. Still dreaming of Polish independence, Kosciuszko traveled to France but failed to secure an alliance with Napoleon, and he ended up in Switzerland where he died in 1817. The current exhibit is recreated from an inventory found in Thomas Jefferson's personal papers.

Highlights:

A ceremonial tomahawk presented to Kosciuszko by Chief Little Turtle of the Miami Indian nation

Kosciuszko's sable fur, featured in Jefferson's famous portrait

Todd House

343 Walnut Street (Map No. 1)
215-965-2305
www.nps.gov/inde/todd-house.html

Open: Daily; Ranger tours only

Admission: Adults, $2.00; Children, Free. Tickets obtained at the visitor center (corner of 6th & Market Streets) for a combined one-hour tour with the Bishop White House (see above).

Although this Georgian house is named for its first owner, John Todd, he is merely an interesting footnote to the real historic interest of the site. After Mr. Todd and one of their sons died of yellow fever in the great epidemic of 1793, his widow Dolley was introduced to up-and-coming politician James Madison by Aaron Burr. Indeed, it is believed that the pair first met in the parlor of this middle-class home where Dolley lived with her surviving son, her brother and sister, and law clerks who worked for Todd's legal practice. The house retains its aspect of the home of a professional man in the late eighteenth century.

Highlights:
A reproduction of John Todd's legal office
An eighteenth-century flower garden
A parlor interpretation to reflect the tastes of less austere Quakers

University of Pennsylvania Museum of Archaeology and Anthropology

3260 South Street (Map No. 2)

215-898-4000

www.museum.upenn.edu

Open: Tu–Sa, 10:00 AM–4:30 PM; Su, 1:00 PM–5:00 PM (Sep.–May only)

Admission: Adults, $8.00; Children 6–17, $5.00; Seniors and Students, Free

As a sponsor for more than 100 years of some of the most important archaeological expeditions the world over, the Museum of Archaeology and Anthropology has amassed a truly stunning collection of nearly one million objects from the ancient and modern cultures of the world. One of the most important museums of its type in the country, its collection includes an extensive array of Near Eastern artifacts dating to 4500 BC (some now unique after the destruction of the national museum in Iraq) as well as artifacts from Mesoamerica, Africa, Europe, Polynesia, and the Far East. Permanent galleries include presentations of Ancient Egyptian culture, complete with a world-class display of the mummification process of animals and humans, the Ancient Greek and Roman worlds, Native Americans of the southwest and northwest, and materials related to the history of Buddhism. The museum's collection of Chinese art and artifacts is located in a rotunda that reaches 90 feet high, one of the largest unsupported masonry domes in America. The Africa exhibit highlights the diversity and richness of material arts from that continent. Don't miss the Etruscan gallery, with the most comprehensive collection in the United States, where visitors can hear a portion of Etruscan texts being read, a unique opportunity to listen to an extinct language that is unrelated to any living language family. The museum is an active host for national and international traveling exhibits that complement the museum's permanent displays.

Highlights:

A crystal ball once owned by China's dowager empress

The famous Mesopotamian sculpture, *Ram in the Thicket*, and other Ur artifacts

Native American tools

A scale model of a Roman house

United States Mint

151 N. Independence Mall East (Map No. 1)
215-408-0112
www.usmint.gov/mint_tours

Hours: Please call in advance for a tour
Admission: Free

On April 2, 1792, the United States Congress passed the coinage act, which created a national mint and authorized construction of a mint building in Philadelphia, the nation's capitol. America's first circulating coins were minted here—11,178 copper cents, which were delivered in March 1793. Soon after, gold and silver coins were struck and circulated. Legend has it that President Washington, who lived only a few blocks from the new Mint, donated some of his own silver for the minting. The Mint has been moved from its original building at 7th and Arch Streets and is now a short walk from the Liberty Bell. The current facility produces circulating coins of all denominations (half of those in national circulation, in fact), commemorative coins, and dies for stamping coins and medals. As one of only two United States Mint facilities in the country that allow public tours, it is well worth calling ahead and scheduling a visit.

Highlights:
An original coining press used in 1792
Modern coin-making machinery that runs 24 hours a day
Rare and historic American coins

Wagner Free Institute of Science

1700 W. Montgomery Avenue (Map No. 2)

215-763-6529

www.wagnerfreeinstitute.org

Open: Tu–F, 9:00 AM–4:00 PM

Admission: Free

Who said there aren't time machines? Step into the Wagner Free Institute of Science and you are transported back to a world of Victorian curiosity. Here is a natural history museum—a genuine national treasure—that has remained fundamentally unchanged since the late nineteenth century. Many of its display cases, even its labels, are from the era of the founder, William Wagner. Visitors view specimens in a graduated manner, starting with very simple life forms and progressing to complex ones. With more than 100,000 specimens on display, ranging from shells to mastodon teeth and stuffed animals, a visit here is an educational experience indeed, which was the intent of the institute in the first place: free public science education. The museum, a National Historic Landmark building, was built in 1865 by the same architect who created City Hall. The Wagner continues to provide free public lectures on science, and the museum should be on the list of anyone interested in the history of science, Victorian culture, or the experience of something out of the ordinary.

Highlights:

A vast collection of American and European fossils

A complete skeleton of an English draft horse

A skull of the first saber-tooth tiger found in North America

Woodford

33rd & Dauphin Streets, Fairmount Park East (Map No. 2)
215-229-6115
www.philamuseum.org/collections/parkhouse/woodford.shtml

Open: Tu–Su, 10:00 AM–4:00 PM
Admission: $3.00

One of the earliest surviving examples of late Georgian architecture in Philadelphia, and considered by many the finest, Woodford is an elegant two-story brick country home finished by its second owner sometime in the 1770s. The house was also witness to the realities of Philadelphia history: the first owner was a friend and confidante of Benjamin Franklin, while a subsequent owner was a staunch Tory who saw Woodford confiscated after the Revolution. Throughout the history of its ownership, which includes the Wharton family, the house has always been an example of an elegant lifestyle. The exquisite furnishings, so much at home here, are the estate of Naomi Wood, a noted collector of American furniture and decorative arts. Woodford was recently damaged by fire, but fortunately no major loss was incurred, and the house is scheduled to reopen shortly.

Highlights:
A mahogany desk and bookcase attributed to John Elliot
A pediment mantle from 1750
A second-floor three-part Venetian window

Woodmere Art Museum

9201 Germantown Avenue (Map No. 3)
215-247-0476
www.woodmereartmuseum.org

Open: Tu–Sa, 10:00 AM–5:00 PM; Su, 1:00 PM–5:00 PM
Admission: Adults, $5.00; Seniors and Students, $3.00

In the genteel Chestnut Hill section of Philadelphia stands the
Woodmere Museum, a nineteenth-century stone Victorian man-
sion on six acres. Showcasing the art of the Philadelphia area, the
Woodmere collection contains works by major artists like Daniel
Garber, Benjamin West, and N. C. Wyeth. The Woodmere Art
Museum is also very active in art education, sponsoring cultural
tours, lectures, studio art classes, and a concert series in its own
Catherine Kuch Rotunda Gallery. Designed to "celebrate
Philadelphia's artistic legacy"—which it does in impressive
style—the core collection and the museum building itself are a
gift of the philanthropist Charles Knox Smith, who had worked
his way up from an oil driver to an oil magnate, ultimately making Woodmere his home.

Highlights:
Benjamin West's *The Fatal Wounding of Sir Philip Sidney*
Edward Redfield's *Later Afternoon (Delaware River)*
Daniel Garber's *Spring Valley Inn*

The Wood Turning Center

501 Vine Street (Map No. 1)
215-923-8000
www.woodturningcenter.org

Open: M–F, 10:00 AM–5:00 PM; Sa, noon–5:00 PM
Admission: Free

A Philadelphia institution for more than 20 years, the Wood
Turning center has inhabited this Old City site for the last few
years. A celebration of the creative potential of using a turning
device or lathe to create art objects and tools, the center com-
prises a permanent collection and a gallery dedicated to this
ancient process (the oldest turned object is a prehistoric wooden
bowl found in an Irish bog). Despite the name, the center also
showcases pieces in metals, plastics, and other media malleable to
the technique of turning, as well as elaborately carved and painted objects that were initially shaped on a lathe. Be prepared to be
surprised at the breadth of imagination used by contemporary
artists as they borrow an age-old technique.

Wyck

6026 Germantown Pike (Map No. 3)
215-848-1690
www.wyck.org

Open: Tu & Th, noon–4:30 PM; Sa, 1:00 PM–4:00 PM (Apr. 1–Dec. 13)
Admission: Adults, $5.00; Seniors and Students, $4.00; Families,
$10.00

Owned by the same family for nearly 300 years, Wyck is a verita-
ble time capsule of how well-to-do Quakers lived from the seventeenth to the late nineteenth century. America's history has
touched the house as well—it was a field hospital during the
Battle of Germantown and in 1825, the site of a reception for
General Lafayette. Each of the nine generations of the Wistar-
Haines family placed its own stamp on the architecture and
holdings of the house, most importantly in the early nineteenth
century when the family hired architect William Strickland who
recast the house's interior layout to maximize their living space,
turning what was essentially two smaller structures held together
by a covered breezeway into the single house we know today.
The furnishings and decorations in this National Historic
Landmark are those collected by the family and are distinctive for
what they can tell the visitor about the idiosyncratic tastes of
succeeding generations, and the changing economic and social
times in which they lived.

Highlights:
One of the oldest continuously cultivated rose gardens in
America
The main dining room with the very rare Tucker porcelain din-
ner service on display

Appendix

The following lists are thematic guides to the collections of the museums in Philadelphia. All lists are in alphabetical order.

Ten Essential Museums

Academy of Natural Sciences

Carpenters' Hall

Cliveden of the National Trust

Elfreth's Alley

Franklin Court

Franklin Institute

Historic Bartram's Garden

Independence National Historical Park (Secured Area)

Philadelphia Museum of Art

University of Pennsylvania Museum of Archaeology and Anthropology

Only in Philadelphia

Betsy Ross House

Eastern State Penitentiary Historic Site

Elfreth's Alley

Fabric Workshop

Franklin Court

Independence National Historical Park (Secured Area)

Mummers Museum

Mütter Museum

National Constitution Center

Philadelphia Beauty Showcase National Historical Museum

Philadelphia Insectarium

Rodin Museum

Ten Museums for Children

Academy of Natural Sciences
Betsy Ross House
Fireman's Hall
Fort Mifflin
Franklin Institute
Independence National Historical Park (Secured Area)
Independence Seaport Museum
Philadelphia Insectarium
Please Touch Museum
University of Pennsylvania Museum of Archaeology and Anthropology

Ten Museums for Teenagers

Eastern State Penitentiary Historic Site
Federal Reserve Bank "Money in Motion"
Franklin Institute
Independence National Historical Park (Secured Area)
Independence Seaport Museum
Johnson House Historic Site
Mütter Museum
Philadelphia Museum of Art
University of Pennsylvania Museum of Archaeology and Anthropology
Wagner Free Institute of Science

Ten Museums — Art & Architecture

Athenaeum of Philadelphia
Cliveden of the National Trust
Drexel University Museums
Ebenezer Maxwell Mansion
Glen Foerd
LaSalle University Art Museum
Pennsylvania Academy of the Fine Arts
Philadelphia Museum of Art
Rosenbach Museum and Library
Strawberry Mansion

Ten Museums — American History

Civil War Library and Museum
Deshler-Morris House
Elfreth's Alley Museum
Fort Mifflin
Historic Rittenhouse Town
Independence National Historical Park (Secured Area)
Independence Seaport Museum
Johnson House Historic Site
Pennsylvania Hospital
Powel House

Ten Museums — Military History

Carpenters' Hall
Civil War Library and Museum
Cliveden of the National Trust
Deshler-Morris House
Fort Mifflin
Grand Army of the Republic Museum
Independence Seaport Museum
New Hall Military Museum
Philadelphia Museum of Art (arms & armor collection)
Thaddeus Kosciuszko National Memorial

Ten Museums — Regional Interest

Atwater Kent Museum of Philadelphia
Carpenters' Hall
Eastern State Penitentiary Historic Site
Franklin Court
Germantown Historical Society
Historic Rittenhouse Town
Johnson House Historic Site
Mummers Museum
Pennsylvania Academy of the Fine Arts
SEPTA Museum

Ten Museums — Science & Technology

Academy of Natural Sciences
American Philosophical Society
Edwin and Trudy Weaver Historical Dental Museum
Franklin Institute
Historic Bartram's Garden
Mütter Museum
Pennsylvania Hospital
Philadelphia Insectarium
Physick House
Wagner Free Institute of Science

Religious-related Museums

Arch Street Friends Meeting House
Free Quaker Meeting House
Historic St. George's United Methodist Church
Mennonite Meetinghouse
Mother Bethel African Methodist Episcopal Church
National Museum of American Jewish History
Philadelphia Museum of Judaica at Rodeph Shalom
Presbyterian Historical Society

House Museums and Museums with Historic Houses

Belmont Mansion
Betsy Ross House
Bishop White House
Cedar Grove
Cliveden of the National Trust
Declaration (Graff) House
Deshler-Morris House
Ebenezer Maxwell Mansion
Edgar Allen Poe National Historic Site
Elfreth Alley Museum
Glen Foerd
Grumblethorpe
Historic Bartram's Garden
Historic Rittenhouse Town
Johnson House Historic Site
Laurel Hill
Lemon Hill
Marian Anderson Historical Residence and Museum
Mount Pleasant
Paul Robeson House
Physick House
Powel House
Rittenhouse Town
Rosenbach Museum and Library
Robert W. Ryerss Library and Museum
Shofuso
Stenton
Strawberry Mansion
Sweetbrier
Todd House
Woodford
Wyck

Museums that Require Appointments

Athenaeum of Philadelphia*
CIGNA Museum and Art Collection
Concord School House
Edwin and Trudy Weaver Historical Dental Museum
Germantown Historical Society*
Glen Foerd
Living Loft Puppet Museum
Marian Anderson Historical Residence and Museum
Mennonite Meetinghouse
Mother Bethel African Methodist Episcopal Church
Paul Robeson House
Philadelphia Beauty Showcase National Historical Museum
Philadelphia Contributionship for the Insurance of Houses from Loss by Fire*
Philadelphia University–The Design Center
Romanian Folk Art Museum
Shoe Museum
Stephen Girard Collection
United States Mint

*For additional tours of special exhibits or collections only

Index of Alternative Museum Names

Bartram's Garden, *see* Historic Bartram's Garden

Burholme, *see* The Robert W. Ryerss Library and Museum

Congress Hall, *see* Independence National Historical Park

Dental Museum, *see* Edwin and Trudy Weaver Historical Dental Museum

Design Center, *see* Philadelphia University–The Design Center

Dilworth House, *see* Todd House

Doll Museum, *see* Philadelphia Doll Museum

Flag Museum, *see* Betsy Ross House

Girard Collection, *see* Stephen Girard Collection

Graff House, *see* Declaration House

Independence Hall, *see* Independence National Historical Park

Insectarium, *see* Philadelphia Insectarium

Japanese House and Garden, *see* Shofuso

Kosciuszko Museum, *see* Thaddeus Kosciuszko National Memorial

Liberty Bell, *see* Independence National Historical Park

Maxwell Mansion, *see* Ebenezer Maxwell Mansion

Museum of American Art, *see* Pennsylvania Academy of the Fine Arts

Museum of American Jewish History, *see* National Museum of American Jewish History

Museum of Archaeology and Anthropology, *see* University of Pennsylvania Museum of Archaeology and Anthropology

Museum of Judaica, *see* Philadelphia Museum of Judaica at Rodeph Shalom

Nursing Museum, *see* History of Nursing Museum

Puppet Museum, *see* Living Loft Puppet Museum

Rittenhouse Town, *see* Historic Rittenhouse Town

St. George's United Methodist Church, *see* Historic St. George's United Methodist Church

Swedish Museum, *see* American Swedish Historical Museum

Westphal Picture Gallery, *see* Drexel University Museums